MARIAH CAREY

THE UNAUTHORIZED BIOGRAPHY

D1609388

MARIAH CAREY

THE UNAUTHORIZED BIOGRAPHY

Marc Shapiro

ECW PRESS

The publication of *Mariah Carey* has been generously supported
by the Government of Canada through the
Book Publishing Industry Development Program.

CANADIAN CATALOGUING IN PUBLICATION DATA
Shapiro, Marc, 1949-
Mariah Carey: the unauthorized biography
Includes bibliographical references.
ISBN 1-55022-444-1
1. Carey, Mariah. 2. Singers - United States - Biography. I. Title.
ML420.C2333S52 2001 782.42164'092 C00-933281-2

Front cover photo by Mark Allen/Globe Photos.
Back cover photo by Kevin Mazur/London Features.
Cover by Guylaine Régimbald - SOLO DESIGN.
Copyediting by Focus Strategic Communications Inc.
Typesetting by Yolande Martel.
This book is set in Sari and Malaise.

Printed by Transcontinental.

Distributed in Canada by General Distribution Services,
325 Humber College Boulevard, Etobicoke, Ontario M9W 7C3.

Distributed in the United States by LPC Group,
1436 West Randolph Street, Chicago, IL 60607, U.S.A.

Distributed in Europe by Turnaround Publisher Services, Unit 3,
Olympia Trading Estate, Coburg Road, Wood Green, London, N2Z 6T2.

Distributed in Australia and New Zealand by Wakefield Press,
17 Rundle Street (BOX 2266), Kent Town, South Australia 5071.

Published by ECW PRESS
Suite 200
2120 Queen Street East
Toronto, Ontario M4E 1E2
Canada.

ecwpress.com

PRINTED AND BOUND IN CANADA

TABLE OF CONTENTS

FOREWORD

There are a few things you will not read in *Mariah Carey: The Unautho-rized Biography*. The first is reviews. If you weren't there screaming your lungs out in the front row as Mariah put you through the emotional ringer with her soulful ballads and electrifying dance numbers, you don't need a disembodied third party telling you what you missed — because you already know. The reason you love Mariah Carey and her music is personal and individual. You don't need a reviewer who got a free record telling you why you paid real money for the privilege of entering a lifelong love affair with her music and her groove. You also won't get a whole lot of studio gab, techno theory, and gossip about the dollars and cents and behind-the-scenes deal-making that would be of interest only to bean counters and number crunchers. Why? Because the fantasy is what is important in this picture. Anything else is just useless clutter.

What you will get in this book is the fairy tale, the Cinderella story — the things that bring a smile to your face, tears to your eyes, and fill you with hope for the future. We've all heard this story before. It's your classic rags-to-riches tale, but since when are happy endings such a bad thing? Since when did it become a crime for nice people to win out in the end? Guess what? It's not. I dig 'em. And I'm sure you do, too.

Mariah Carey's story is about the things that make us believe that if it can happen for her, there's a chance for the rest of us, too. Because Mariah Carey, despite all the naysayers over the years, is not a prefab byproduct of some big, faceless pop music machine. We all know what those are like, and we can spot them a mile away. There is humanity in the life and times of Mariah Carey. There is soul in her voyage of self-discovery. And, finally, there is reality in the disappointments, the hard knocks, and ultimate triumphs of the creative spirit that have gone into making Mariah Carey the consummate superstar and the all-too-human being we love. Music has been Mariah Carey's life. But what you'll discover as you flip through the pages of *Mariah Carey* is that there is more to the story. So much more.

Mariah did not grow up in a fairy tale world. Her family was anything but normal and there was a lot of turmoil, perhaps too much for a child so young. To salve the discomfort, Mariah turned to her one solace — music — and in many instances, it was a balm for the emotional hurts in her world. In a sense, it was also her shortcut to the adult world. Her acquaintances were primarily much older than she was, in many cases adults, and because of that, Mariah often found herself whipping through those Kodak moments of youth with hardly any time to stop and experience what it was like to just play like a normal kid. Literally and figuratively, music had guided Mariah into the working world, and in later years, there would be a cost.

While wise beyond her years when it came to her music, Mariah continued to remain very much the naive child well into her adult years, often seemingly no better equipped than the average teenager to deal with life outside the cocoon of the recording studio. Consequently, at a time when she should have been standing strong and fighting for her creative rights, she was allowing herself to be molded and shaped into something she sensed was not really her, but she was too inexperienced to defend herself against this force.

Music had also, to a large extent, deprived her of a well-rounded personal life. It made her smart about her love and sexuality, which was good. But it stunted her socially and blurred her emotions when it came to affairs of the heart. It is easy in hindsight to argue that some of her romantic choices were mistakes, but in her mind, at the time, she felt that she was doing the right thing. As a consequence, it wasn't until she was in her mid-twenties that Mariah was suddenly faced with having to learn the ins and outs of the dating game, essentially for the first time. A normal teenage life might have prepared her for all this.

Fortunately Mariah has been a quick study, and once again, music and song have been her guiding light. Finally asserting herself after nearly a decade of creative repression and frustration, she has emerged her own woman on all fronts. Musically, she has divested herself of even a hint of manipulation and has reached back into her youth, to the music that poured out of radios and record-player speakers and made her want to sing in the first place. The music, now more than ever, is truly hers.

Mariah Carey has never rushed into anything, preferring a slow and deliberate approach to her music as well as her life rather than one spontaneous leap. Her decisions have not always been the popular or expedient ones, and she has never taken the easy way out, which is why she has often been at odds with those who have guided her professional life. But you have to applaud anyone who takes even a small step away from conventional wisdom, and that is why we give kudos to Mariah.

Personally she is also in a better place. She has had the requisite failed relationship that played out in the glare of the media and she has survived it. And she was finally mature enough to find and accept what, at least to this point, is a true and lasting relationship. It has taken thirty years, but Mariah Carey has finally taken her music and her life to the adult world. It is a place where shifting loyalties make for an ever-changing landscape in which you are only as good as your last hit record. That was never truer than now, but amid all the turmoil, Mariah and her music continue to stand tall, pushing the envelope at every turn and proving, with each album and sold-out concert performance, that there is truly a place in the often raucous world of popular music for a little style and elegance.

She is an adult with a definite agenda. Her life has always been defined by music and song. Even as a child, there was drive and focus in the pursuit of her dream. Nothing was going to stop her and nobody was going to dissuade her. And in the end, this goal proved to be a two-edged sword. But Mariah has emerged every bit the battle-scarred survivor. Her music has proven her sword and shield in her battles to be an individual. It is a battle she has won.

Mariah's story is ongoing and like all good tales, the future will doubtless hold many surprises and passions. Her musical aspirations know no bounds, and her loyal following, numbering in the millions, seems ready to take the ride with her. And one thing is certain; all the things that have gone into forging the life that has been Mariah Carey to this point will have a mighty impact on how this multitalented performer meets the future.

The future is now. So is the past. Get ready for a wild ride.

Marc Shapiro — April 2001

PROLOGUE

On the surface, it seemed like a typical Mariah Carey night — lots of stuff was happening. Earlier on, Mariah, dressed to the nines in the current hot fashions, walked onto the stage amid thunderous applause to accept the Artist of the Decade Award at the prestigious Billboard Music Award ceremony held in the appropriately glitzy Las Vegas. There had been many awards over the years (and not a few slights), and Mariah had come to take them all in stride. But being named Artist of the Decade really meant something. It was kind of a validation for a meteoric rise to stardom that had, by the end of the nineties, resulted in more than 100 million records sold worldwide, a series of soldout, critically praised concerts, and a reputation as one of the sweetest voices in pop and soul.

You don't get to be Artist of the Decade for being a one-hit wonder or the flavor of the month. And during the decade 1990-2000, the ever-changing face of music made both of those titles commonplace. But Mariah was different. She was one of a very small handful of artists who transcended the trends, turning out consistent, commercial music that captured the ears of record buyers no matter what form of music was in vogue.

Mariah had prided herself in being very much the adult. But as she held back the tears and accepted the award, it was not hard to see the little girl in her face — a little girl who had experienced a lot. . . .

CHAPTER ONE

Welcome to the World

Life in County Cork, Ireland has never been easy. It was the rare child who went beyond high school. Rarer still was the person who did not wind up toiling as a farmer or in the mills and factories that dotted the admittedly attractive landscape of forests and rolling flatlands. Patricia Hickey's father was the exception to the rule. He had grown up with music in his heart and song in his soul. His parents noticed their son's budding talents at an early age and saw it as a way for him to have a better life. They encouraged him, and he grew into a singer and musician of some note.

Over the years, he managed to carve out a reasonable living and soon married. Not long after, his wife found herself pregnant. The months leading up to Patricia Hickey's birth were a time of important decisions for the couple. Patricia's father had gone as far as he could as a working musician in his native Ireland, and he reasoned that his talents would go farther and be much more lucrative in the United States. There, singer-songwriters were making a comeback with the postwar renaissance of folk music. Through hard work and perseverance, the couple had saved up enough to finance the dream of moving to the United States and what they believed would be a better life. And so it was that Mrs. Hickey, heavy with child, and her husband made the sea crossing that would eventually find them settling in Springfield, Illinois. Unfortunately, the stress and strain of a hard life unexpectedly caught up with Mr. Hickey, and he died a month before Patricia was born. Patricia's mother was resilient. She soon recovered from the loss of her husband and the fear of being alone in a strange land. By all accounts, she raised her daughter in the conservative Midwest environment that was Springfield on a steady diet of church learning and traditional family values.

Patricia grew up a bright, precocious child, quick with questions and in her element as the creator of imaginary games. She made friends easily, but, as her mother discovered, she could also be quite content by herself. Patricia had never known her father but apparently had inherited his musical gifts: at a very early age, she could quite naturally sing in clear, resonant tones. The young girl became a regular in all high-school musical activities. While she flirted with the typical teenage passions for rock and soul music, Patricia was instinctively drawn to the dramatic world of opera. Her mother strongly believed that her daughter's future lay in a life of music and did not stand in her way when, at age seventeen, shortly after her graduation from high school, Patricia announced that she was going to New York to make her way as a singer.

New York in the late fifties was an exciting place to be. Broadway was on fire with traditional and experimental theater and music of all kinds, and Patricia fell in love with the sights and sounds of that fascinating city. The young woman had her moments of doubt as she contemplated a musical life in New York, but she knew that she was in the right place and that something wonderful would most assuredly happen. There was no logic in her thinking — just abiding faith in a fantasy and the belief that anything was possible. It was New York, after all! Following the inevitable period of dues-paying and minimum-wage jobs, Patricia auditioned for and was accepted by the prestigious New York City Opera company. Not long after this, Alfred Roy Carey entered her life.

Carey, of African and Venezuelan parentage, had been, like Patricia, brought up in a strict, no-nonsense household. In Venezuela, his family name had been Nunes, but like so many others who immigrated to the United States in the late forties and early fifties, Alfred's father Americanized his name to Carey because it was easy to pronounce. He felt the new name would open the door to success for the Nunes family. Apparently he was right because after some initial struggles, the family prospered sufficiently to allow young Alfred to go to college where he put his love of math and science to good use, becoming an aeronautical engineer.

While Patricia was creative and free-spirited, Alfred was detail-oriented and analytical. As it turned out, it was a classic case of opposites attracting.

And it was Alfred's analytical side that led to long discussions about what the reality of their life as an interracial married couple would be for them and for their children if their relationship turned serious. Their love overcame any fears, and after a relatively short courtship, Alfred and Patricia were married in New York City in 1960.

The early 1960s were a period of growing racial equality in the United States. It was the era of Martin Luther King Jr. and the civil rights movement. It was a time when blacks began moving from the back of the bus and making strides toward equality by registering to vote. Everything from schools to lunch counters was being integrated. Unfortunately, racially mixed couples continued to bring out long-held prejudices from blacks and whites alike. A cloud of anger and intolerance would dog the marriage of Alfred and Patricia Carey. "My parents had a lot of strikes against them just being an interracial couple," Mariah told *Jet* magazine. "There was a lot of racism in the sixties and seventies. My brother and sister and I were the products of forbidden love."

Years later, Mariah would recall tales of the racial bigotry her parents had experienced in the years before she was born. "From the start, my mother's family basically disowned her when she married my father," she once tearfully explained to Oprah Winfrey. "Her mother made her pretend she wasn't married. When she came to family events, she had to come alone and pretend she was single. All sorts of crazy things happened. Their car got blown up, and their dogs were poisoned." But the newly married couple had a bit of the crusader about them and were determined to overcome these attitudes. Rather than living in a more ethnically diverse city, they chose to meet their problems head-on by attempting to make a life for themselves in all-white suburban communities that dotted upstate New York and Rhode Island. "When they moved to an all-white neighborhood, my mother had to buy the house because the owners would not sell if they knew she had a black husband." Invariably, however, the hostility of their neighbors would force them to move.

During the first few years of marriage, they moved several times before eventually deciding that racially mixed neighborhoods would be more welcoming. But the same problems would inevitably surface. One night, while her parents sat at the dinner table, somebody fired a bullet through the window, narrowly missing them. Years later, Mariah acknowledged that the racial hatred her parents experienced put added pressure on their marriage despite their best efforts. "It put a strain on their relationship that would never quit," she told *People* magazine. "There was always this tension, and they just fought all the time."

The couple had not been married long when Patricia gave birth to their first child, a son named Morgan. A year later, Allison was born. The Careys brought up their children in much the same way they themselves had been raised. There were rules, and they had to be obeyed. But the strictness was balanced by a loving and open attitude, and this helped them learn to face reality. But despite the fact that the Careys now had a young family, they nevertheless continued their nomadic existence for the next decade, moving back and forth between New York City and nearby Rhode Island in search of peace and a permanent address. Alfred was a hard worker and was always able to provide for his family. Patricia's musical aspirations were sidetracked by the duties of motherhood, but by the late sixties she had resumed her singing career and had advanced to the position of first soloist with the New York City Opera. Occasionally, she would also moonlight as a freelance vocal coach.

By 1968, Alfred and Patricia Carey were fairly settled in their lives and had grudgingly come to accept the racial strife they faced as part of the cost of trying to fit into an unenlightened world. They had long since decided that two children were enough, and so they were more than a bit surprised when Patricia found herself pregnant once again. On March 27, 1970, Mariah Carey was born. She was named after the song "They Call the Wind Mariah" from the 1951 Lerner and Loewe Broadway musical *Paint Your Wagon*. Like her namesake, Mariah, at a very young age, began to exhibit a free-spirited nature that her older siblings did not possess. Mariah was almost instantly captivated by the sound of her mother's operatic voice. Patricia sensed her daughter's interest and, perhaps subconsciously trying to encourage at least one of her children in that direction, made a point of having her youngest daughter around when she rehearsed for the opera or gave voice lessons in her home. And it went without saying that there was always music in the house.

Patricia has often remarked that by the time Mariah was two years old, she was capable of hearing a sound and duplicating it exactly — perfect pitch is a rare talent. However, any doubts that Mariah was anything more than a very good mimic were quickly put to rest. Patricia was rehearsing a song for her performance in an upcoming New York City Opera production of *Rigoletto*. "I missed my cue," she recalled in *People* magazine, "but Mariah didn't. She sang it in Italian, and she was not yet three years old." Mariah proved to be an incredible mimic when it came to songs of any kind, and it was the rare day when the Carey household did not ring with the sound of Mariah marching around the house, singing at the top of her lungs. "Every song that came on the radio, T.V. commercials, I would just sing along with anything I heard," Mariah recalled.

Patricia realized that her daughter had inherited her singing skills, and, while she treated all her children equally, whether consciously or subconsciously, she began to nurture Mariah's talents. She would encourage her daughter to listen in when she was rehearsing and would often end her own sessions by inviting little Mariah to sing along with her. When the two of them were alone during the day, they would continuously break into spontaneous song. Mariah was a willing pupil. "I loved singing," she said in a *Rolling Stone* interview. "I was singing since I started talking." However, her vocal skills sometimes presented a problem in the Carey household. Alfred Carey, while amused and often entertained by his youngest child's singing, was a strict disciplinarian, and one of his most stringent rules was that nobody spoke at the dinner table unless spoken to. This rule was put to the test one day when Mariah burst into song shortly after the family sat down to their evening meal. Her brother and sister were horrified because of the reprimand that would most certainly come. Her father glared at her and barked, "There will be no singing at the table!" Mariah recalled in a *Rolling Stone* interview. "So I got up from the table, went into the living room, got up on the coffee table, and continued singing at the top of my lungs." But her music and singing aspirations were a very private thing for her, and she performed little outside the family home until she was nineteen. Her teachers and friends kidded her about her musical ambition, which only served to make her more inhibited.

Racial problems continued to be a way of life for the Carey family, and, even at an early age, Mariah was aware that they were different and that some people hated difference. "My brother was always getting beaten up," Mariah related to *Eva* magazine. "My sister Allison always got picked on because she had the darkest skin." In fact, Mariah herself escaped relatively unscathed because of her light skin, but she wasn't blind to what was going on around her. The frustration of the intolerance and the constant moves that the family faced had made just getting through each day an ordeal. Tensions in the Carey household continued to escalate. The older Carey children knew there was a lot of unhappiness in the house, but at three, Mariah could not understand why her mother and father were always yelling and why everybody always seemed unhappy. Finally, in 1973, Alfred and Patricia Carey divorced. Allison went to live with her father, while Morgan and Mariah remained with their mother.

The divorce hit three-year-old Mariah particularly hard. In her childlike view of the world, everybody had a mother and father who were always around and there for them. Suddenly, not only was her father gone, but so was her older sister. But the amicable nature of the breakup and the fact that Patricia did not turn her children against their father made the split a little less painful. Initially, Alfred would see his children on a weekly basis, but those visits soon became less frequent and eventually stopped when Alfred got a job in Washington, DC. Mariah has often maintained that she and her father "had a good relationship for about a minute after the divorce," and that she eventually came to terms with this major change in her life. Father and daughter barely keep in touch, but when they do correspond, they are cordial. But the reality was that the divorce hit the young child very hard. She has admitted that the divorce was "a major split for me," and for a long time colored her attitude toward the institution of marriage. "Everybody wishes they had the *Brady Bunch* family," she once said. "But it's not reality."

Life as a single mother was not easy for Patricia Carey. While Alfred paid some child support, there never seemed to be enough money in the Carey household. Her job with the New York City Opera did not pay a great deal, so Patricia was forced to do more and more work as a freelance vocal coach. Despite these problems, Patricia always made sure that the family had some semblance of a normal family life. Mariah would recall that trips to the beach were a favorite outing. The young child loved to frolic among the waves and build sand castles on the shore. Unfortunately her excitement at being at the beach would usually result in a bout of car sickness on the way home.

For Patricia, jobs and rehearsals were often at odd hours of the day and night. Morgan was frequently drafted into babysitting his younger sister but time and again conveniently managed to make himself scarce. Because babysitters cost money, Patricia would often end up bringing Mariah with her. Consequently, at a very early age, Mariah found herself surrounded by singers and musicians in a free-spirited, Bohemian environment. Mariah soaked up the influence and the vibe like a sponge. While other kids her age were singing "Mary Had a Little Lamb," young Mariah was belting out "Satisfaction" by The Rolling Stones. "I enjoyed being around grown-ups as a little kid," Mariah has said. "I would sit around the table with adults and have adult conversations with them."

By the time Mariah turned four, Patricia realized that singing was not just a passing fancy in her daughter's life, and so she began giving Mariah formal lessons. Patricia already had the feeling that her daughter might have what it takes to make it as a professional singer but was nevertheless cautious in encouraging her. However, Mariah did not really need the encouragement — she already knew that singing was what she wanted to do with her life. "Because my mom sang for a living, I knew it could be more than a pipe dream," she told the *New York Times*. "My mom always told me 'You are special. You have talent.' From a very early age, she gave me the belief that I could do this."

Mariah's formal lessons bordered on the informal. Despite being rooted in opera, Patricia made a point of not pushing her daughter in any particular musical direction but rather concentrated her lessons on tone, projection, and the nuts and bolts of singing. Patricia would sit at the piano and hit different notes. Mariah would then have to match the notes with her voice. Eventually, they moved from notes to whole songs. Mariah was a quick study and had perfect pitch. It also didn't hurt that she loved what she was doing.

During those early years, Mariah was exposed to many musical worlds. From her mother she got opera and folk. From her teenage brother who was six years older, and the occasional visits by her sister, she garnered a love for soul and R&B. Al Green, Aretha Franklin, Stevie Wonder, and Gladys Knight were early influences. Through sporadic visits to her paternal grandmother, Mariah discovered the joys of church gospel. But it was Minnie Riperton, the seventies soul singer with her amazing five-to-seven-octave range, who was the overriding influence on Mariah and her own singing style. She remembers the immediate impact that Riperton had on her when Mariah first heard her idol on the radio. Riperton was singing in upper registers that few singers could approach, and Mariah was instantly struck by a style that she considered larger than life. She expressed her enthusiasm to her mother who bought her some of Riperton's records, and

Mariah began practicing in earnest in an attempt to master the singer's technique. Patricia became concerned that her daughter would hurt her vocal cords trying to hit those amazingly high notes. But sounding like Minnie became an obsession for Mariah, and it was not long before her vocal range began to expand to something approximating her idol's style.

But while she was determined in her quest to sound like Minnie Riperton, Mariah always returned to Patricia for those important lessons in music and life. At this point, Patricia had become as much of a friend as a mother. "My mother was very inspirational," she told *Modern Woman* magazine. "She made me feel special and reinforced my belief in myself and my talent." Mariah was aware of lyrics and song structure and was already experimenting in her head with melodies that she heard on the radio. Mariah recalls that she tended to go way overboard with her passion for music and that it would often drive even her supportive mother to distraction. "My mother would have to tear me away from the radio every night just to get me to go to bed," she laughingly recalled. "But then I would sneak back down to the kitchen, bring the radio back into my bedroom, and listen to it under the covers. I used to sing myself to sleep every night."

Along with music instruction, Patricia gave her daughter a healthy dose of self-confidence, self-respect, and independence. These attributes would ultimately allow her to pursue her goal of being a professional singer, but, of more immediate importance, they would allow her to grow up unscathed in what she already perceived as a less-than-normal family environment.

Patricia hated leaving Mariah alone, but she had to go to work, which was often at odd hours. That made it necessary for her to leave Mariah at home with her brother Morgan, but Morgan, being a typical teenager, would promise his mother that he would stay with Mariah and then head for the street corner and his friends the moment she left the house. In those instances, Mariah recalled that the radio would be her babysitter. "I would feel very vulnerable and sometimes scared. I was alone a lot, and so I had time to think. I learned how to be independent."

The Carey's nomadic existence continued. Always one step ahead of the landlord or racist neighbors, Patricia and her children moved with regularity. When they could afford the rent, it was usually a rundown apartment in a questionable part of town. When they could not, Mariah would find herself crashing on a couch or the floor of a friend. With Patricia sometimes working as many as three jobs in a day, Mariah was left to cope by herself with the ever-changing neighborhoods and the friends that would most certainly not be friends for very long. Looking back, Mariah would often acknowledge that part of her insecurities lay in the fact that she could never count on having friends for any length of time. By age five, Mariah Carey was already feeling insecure about a life that always seemed to be about picking up and leaving. "When you live in a middle-class or upper-middle-class neighborhood but you're living in a shack, it just puts you in a weird position." And she would admit in later years that the strain, stress, and anxiety of constantly being uprooted made an indelible impact on her. "I didn't have one neighborhood," she told interviewer Jamie Foster Brown. "We didn't own a house, and we didn't have a lot of money. A lot of times, I did not feel like I fit in. That was a frightening period for me."

She would later recall that a big part of her insecurity growing up was the lack of a true role model. "I felt different from my mother, and I knew I wasn't exactly like my father. I didn't really feel like I had one strong person to relate to." However, her identity crisis did not get in the way of the respect she felt for her mother. In later years, Mariah would often say that what her mother did during that time kept the family afloat and that there was no shame in providing for her family. But instead of becoming withdrawn and unsure, Mariah drew strength from this unconventional and insecure lifestyle, and, by the time she turned six, she was ready to take on the world. She was already exhibiting a restless streak when it came to everyday childhood activities, and she became easily bored at the childish pursuits of her friends. Mariah would recall that she was very aware of her state of mind during those years. "I was like a young adult by age five or six. I was a mature grown-up."

Mariah entered the world of formal education in 1976. At school, she was a shy child, and because she had been constantly uprooted in the early years of her life, she did not make friends easily. Music and the arts were her friends. In fact, they became her passion even at that early age. Mariah would often recall that a preference for creative classes was a constant pattern in her life. "What they used to write on my report card was 'She's very smart but doesn't apply herself unless it's something she likes.'"

Her mother encouraged Mariah to try spreading her creative wings in other areas besides song. She tried her hand at the piano, but the lessons required a degree of concentration and structure that Mariah was not ready

Mariah's junior high photo
CLASSMATES.COM YEARBOOK ARCHIVES

for, and so interest in the instrument soon fell by the wayside. What Mariah found she was quite good at, given her attention to song lyrics, was poetry. She would constantly put her thoughts and feelings down on paper and show them to her mother. Encouraged by the positive feedback, Mariah was overjoyed the day her third-grade teacher, Mr. Cohen, asked the class to write a poem. She felt this was an opportunity for her to stand out from the rest of her class. However her excitement about the writing assignment turned to disappointment when the teacher refused to believe that the poem Mariah had submitted was really her own work and accused her of plagiarism.

Mariah's reputation as an amazing vocalist soon spread through the school district. When the local high-school production of the musical *South Pacific* was looking for a youngster to do the solo on the song "Honey Bun," Mariah, then in the sixth grade, made her singing debut to a packed house. The audience's enthusiastic reaction served to further her ambition to be a performer. That same year, Mariah played the role of Maria in her own sixth-grade class production of *The Sound of Music*.

Mariah's structured school experience was in direct contrast to the free-flowing party atmosphere that often greeted her when she came home. There were always musicians hanging around rehearsing for shows or just jamming. Encouraged by Patricia, Mariah would join in the three-ring circus playing out in her living room. Patricia would beam proudly as her daughter sang to the accompaniment of the adult musicians around her. Mariah's high-octave range had become the talk of this informal group, and more than one person would remark that Mariah already had the talent of a seasoned professional.

However, no matter how insulated and secure she felt in a world of music and song, Mariah could never get away from the real world and its temptations. She learned a hard lesson when her sixteen-year-old sister Allison got pregnant and was forced to get married. Patricia's disappointment in her oldest daughter was obvious, and she reinforced her sense of right and wrong to Mariah. While her mother always took great pains to find the best neighborhoods to live in, Mariah was never far enough from the street to avoid the seamy side of life. Many in her mother's circle predicted privately that Mariah would eventually follow in her sister's footsteps. But music had a stronger hold on her than street life did, and it was her dream of stardom, along with a good measure of luck, that would continue to keep her on the straight and narrow. "I saw a lot of craziness," she once said. "But I made the right decisions by looking at people who made the wrong ones and saying that I would not end up like them."

Mariah had another way of beating the blues. She would spontaneously burst into song. Alone or in a crowd — it did not make a difference. Singing would always bring Mariah back to the good stuff. "I always looked at music as a form of escape," she explained to *VH-1*. "You could be anything you wanted to be when you had music."

Shortly before Mariah turned ten, her mother decided that it was time for her daughter to have some formal instruction in the arts. A local Long Island performing arts center that emphasized music and acting seemed ideal for her. It was expensive, but Patricia felt it was important enough, and so, with the aid of her ex-husband and other family members, she managed to get together the tuition for Mariah to attend the camp for two seven-week sessions during the summers of 1980 and 1981. Mariah recalled that her experience at the camp was important in helping to structure her life and attitude. During her first year, she appeared in the role of Hodel in the musical *Fiddler on the Roof*. In her second year, Mariah was relegated to understudy, but putting the best face on it, she decided that it had at least given her the opportunity to just play and be a kid.

Finally, after years of struggle, Patricia Carey managed to make enough money for a down payment to get her family into a house in the affluent Long Island suburb of Huntington Bay. This was to be their home throughout Mariah's high-school years and beyond. Patricia was working quite regularly now, and this latest move looked to be more permanent. It was 1982, the year that Mariah Carey turned twelve. But to her way of thinking, she had already lived through a lot. "I went through more before the age of twelve than a lot of people go through in their entire lifetime," she said. "My mom's friends would always say that if I made it, it would be a miracle." Mariah had made it this far, but there was more to come — a lot more.

CHAPTER TWO

High School, My School

Mariah Carey already knew what she wanted to do with her life by the time she enrolled in Greenlawn Junior High School near her home in Huntington Bay, and she didn't hesitate to tell people all about her plans. Mariah met Patricia Johnson in her first year of junior high school, and they became close friends during their teen years. Patricia recalled how she and girlfriends would regularly have their ears filled with Mariah's latest, often seemingly exaggerated, plans to be a singer and ultimately a superstar. But while others in Mariah's circle of friends would openly dismiss the youngster's predictions of greatness, money, and having her picture on the cover of every fan magazine, her friend Patricia sensed that Mariah was serious about it and that somehow she would make it happen.

That Mariah felt so strongly at such an early age should not have come as much of a surprise. After all, she had grown up among people who sang and performed for a living and who, by degrees, were successful at what they did. That she could follow in their footsteps was seen as a real possibility in the young girl's eyes. And Patricia Carey sensed that her daughter's life plans would be unshakeable. Deep inside, Patricia was proud but also cautious. She knew firsthand that a career in music was fraught with disappointments and that not everybody could make it to the top. With those realities in mind, Patricia did not deflate Mariah's dreams, but she did warn her with stories of how she had struggled and cautioned her to be prepared. But not wanting to disillusion her daughter, she would reassure Mariah that she felt she had the talent to make it. Mariah liked the sound of that.

With a goal of singing first and foremost in her mind, it was no surprise that Mariah would be less than academically inclined throughout high school. Put quite simply, Mariah loved the classes she was interested in and was bored by everything else. "I was always in the honors creative writing class," the singer told interviewer Jamie Foster Brown. "But then I would go to the worst remedial math class." Patricia Carey knew that school was a constant struggle for her daughter, but, while she insisted that Mariah attend school and do her best in all subjects, she did not demand that she bring home straight As or win honors. By this time, she was well aware that her daughter was going to follow her heart, and so, Patricia was concerned but not overly upset when Mariah did not take her eighth-grade finals. "It's not that I deliberately did not take the finals," Mariah confessed to Rosie O'Donnell. "I always wanted to be prepared for tests, but I was always busy with my music."

Mariah's musical education continued at home. Patricia was not a stage mother and never pushed her daughter. Rather, she gently encouraged her to go where her talent and instincts would take her. When it came to performing in public, Mariah remained hesitant. She would sing for family and friends and, when she was feeling particularly brave, would participate in informal folk-music hoots held in Patricia's home or the home of a musician friend. But for the most part, Mariah's music became a quiet, private place that the young girl would go to. In a sense, Mariah was biding her time. She knew that she was not ready to begin the long, hard climb to the top. But she also knew that someday she would be.

Mariah took the next creative step at age thirteen when she began writing her own songs. Those privy to her early songwriting efforts described Mariah as a songwriter who was skilled beyond her years. She quickly went from doing soul and gospel variations of her favorite singers and songwriters to developing her own original style, heavy into ballads and love songs that borrowed liberally from her real-life experiences. In fact, a preview of things to come was the young girl's uncanny ability to take her teenage insecurities and put them into words. Patricia, who would inevitably be the sounding board for those early songwriting efforts, was impressed because even at this early stage, Mariah could write big, booming, emotional ballads. But Patricia saw much more in her daughter's talents than singing and songwriting. In her expressive, animated nature and sense of drama, she also saw her potential as an actress. She encouraged her daughter's participation in local acting workshops, in which Mariah showed a great deal of promise — so much so that Patricia decided to take her daughter to New York City to audition for parts in Broadway musicals. Initially, Mariah was a bit shy about the audition process and with having to compete against more experienced child actors. But she eventually became comfortable with the procedure. During this period, Mariah auditioned for the role of Annie in the Broadway play but lost out because she was too tall. Although Mariah never actually landed a role, the excitement of going through auditions and playing the part of actress were positive experiences for her.

Mariah's junior high-school years were much more normal than her obsessional prepping for a career in music would lead us to believe. There were the early pressures of puberty that included an increased anxiety regarding her looks and all the other things that young girls go through. In that sense, Mariah fit right in — insecurities and all. "I always thought I was ugly," she told *Seventeen* magazine. "My best friend was this perfect-looking blonde, and there I was with all this frizzy hair and bushy eyebrows. I remember being in the seventh grade and really wanting to impress this guy, so I tried highlighting my hair but it came out all orange." Mariah's early romances were mostly crushes, never serious. There was hand-holding and a kiss on the cheek, but she was a bit shy around boys and preferred to hang out in groups rather than forming individual friendships.

In 1984, Mariah entered Harborfields High School. She was changing both emotionally and personally. She was more confident and outgoing, and as she began to come out of her shell, her circle of friends grew.

But Mariah's attitude toward formal education remained the same. "I always wanted to graduate from high school so I could get on with my life," she recalled in an *US* magazine interview. "But I always felt like I was wasting my time because I knew I wanted to be a singer." While she had a good time socially in high school, Mariah did not participate in any extra-curricular music activities. "I thought I was too cool to do anything related to school activities," she said in a *Vibe* magazine interview. But she was outgoing and self-confident, which contributed to her getting the nickname Miss Mod. But the reality was that Mariah was very much the chameleon during her school years. "I went through a lot of different stages," she related in *Dolly* magazine. "For a while, I distanced myself from a lot of kids. From the seventh grade on, I was the tough girl. I used to slam the cheerleaders into lockers and stuff like that. I wasn't really bad. I was just acting tough."

What she was was very normal. She would hang out with friends, go to parties and, despite her mother's wary eye, Mariah had several boyfriends. A persistent rumor in later years was that one of Mariah's high-school suitors was actually a much older drug dealer and that she often found herself hanging out with a dangerous crowd. But given Patricia's vigilance, that would appear unlikely. In the tenth grade, one of Mariah's high-school crushes presented her with a keepsake, which turned out to be her "lucky" ring, one that she not only has kept all these years but wears every time she performs. What Mariah remembers about her early high-school romantic attachments was that they were casual and fleeting. Mariah, despite peer pressure and her galloping hormones, managed to remain a virgin throughout high school. "I always had these older boyfriends since I was thirteen," she revealed in *Rolling Stone*. "But I didn't really do anything with them. I had relationships, but I did nothing. I was very virginal, and people wouldn't have thought so because I was always walking around with these tight-ass jeans on." When it came to her virtue and sexual matters, she learned from those around her. She knew about girls who, like her sister Allison, had become pregnant, dropped out of school, and ruined their lives. And when she had those expected lapses in judgment, she could always count on her mother to rein her in.

Steve Park got to know Mariah in high school through his girlfriend. He described her as "kind of quiet but really nice." He remembered that they would often get together and just drive around and hang out. But he also recalled that when they would swing by Mariah's house, they would often run up against her mother. "Her mom was real strict," said Steve. "There would be times when we would try and get Mariah to go out with us, but she couldn't because her mother would always insist that her singing lessons came first. I remember feeling sorry for her."

By the age of fourteen, Mariah Carey had begun living her dream. Through word of mouth and her mother's contacts, she became a much-in-demand demo singer for a number of Long Island recording studios. Demo singers record songs for songwriters, who can then present their material to music publishers and other singers. However, Mariah would often get in trouble doing these sessions because, with an already well-developed sense of songwriting, she would inevitably find fault with the songs she was

Mariah in her senior year

CLASSMATES.COM YEARBOOK ARCHIVES

singing and attempt to change the lyrics. The jobs brought much-needed money into the Carey household, but, more importantly, it was an eye-opening introduction to the mysterious world of the recording studio. But Mariah felt as if she were in her element and had no problem with this totally adult-dominated environment. Things were on a more professional level, and she was instantly drawn to the process of making music. This was truly the beginning of Mariah's real education.

By her junior year in high school, her lack of interest in formal studies and her increasing absences from class (which earned her a new nickname, Mirage) became a subject of concern to the school administration. James Malone, her high-school guidance counselor, encouraged her to pursue her singing dream, but, at the same time, he insisted that she develop more marketable skills that she could fall back on in the event her music career stalled. Likewise, the school's assistant vice-principal, John Garvey, spent many futile hours trying to get Mariah to buckle down and study. But, as he explained in a *New York Newsday* article, it was to no avail. "You could talk to her until you were blue in the face, and it didn't do any good. When you talked to her about it, she'd let you know it just wasn't that important in her life because she was going to be a rock star. She was fully convinced it was going to happen. Nothing was going to stand in her way."

In a 1994 *Jet* magazine conversation, Mariah recalled those talks with school staff members, and while she understood that it was their job to encourage children to follow their dreams, she resented the fact that they were trying to step on hers. Nevertheless, she did not blame them for trying to keep her from dropping out of school. "I didn't blame them for trying to encourage me to do better scholastically because they never saw me sing. They just saw this kid who had this dream of making music and being a singer." But the constant urging of her school teachers to learn something that she could "fall back on" finally made an impression, and beginning in her junior year, Mariah began to study beauty and cosmetics. Mariah got a kick out of doing something that a lot of her friends were doing, but she never really took it that seriously.

Word of Mariah's demo work and reports of her emerging talents as a songwriter had spread throughout the informal Huntington Bay music community, and she soon hooked up with aspiring songwriter Gavin Christopher. This was truly a big step for Mariah who, up to that point, had seen music as a solitary endeavor. That she would consider taking suggestions and criticism from another person was a definite sign of maturity. The quality of the songs that Mariah and Gavin produced on their crude recording equipment was truly impressive. They were lyrically strong and emotionally mature compositions that compared favorably with much of the music that was being played at the time on the radio. And although none of these efforts ever amounted to much, they were instrumental in getting her started. One of her most ardent supporters, after her mother of course, was her older brother Morgan, who, despite his constant battle with cerebral palsy, was attempting a career of his own as a musician and producer. Morgan had always been a quiet supporter of his sister's musical aspirations, but he stepped forward in a major way when Mariah turned sixteen. He put up the money to record a professional-quality demo of her songs in a Manhattan recording studio. For Mariah, Morgan's generous gift continued to open her eyes to the wonders of the professional music world. She was barely old enough to get a driver's license, but there she was, surrounded by professional musicians who were playing her songs. Mariah's past insecurities surfaced early in the sessions, and she was tentative in the face of much older, seasoned players. But she soon realized that this was *her* show, and her confidence returned. For their part, the musicians were immediately drawn to the young girl's enthusiasm, her multioctave voice, and her passionate songs.

Now, Patricia Carey was caught on the horns of a dilemma. She insisted that Mariah study and graduate high school, but she was overjoyed at the opportunity the recording experience offered her daughter. At the same time, she was worried that this new temptation would lure Mariah to drop out of school. She gave her blessing to Mariah's demo sessions but insisted that Mariah would somehow have to fit school into her busy schedule. Mariah recalled, in *Ebony*, how she was able to balance both. "After school, I would commute to Manhattan to work all night with musicians. I usually would not get home until 3 A.M., get up at 7 A.M. to go to school. And I would always be late."

By this time, songwriting partner Gavin Christopher had gone on to other things, leaving music for good, and Mariah was once again writing by herself. But that didn't last long. One day, Mariah discovered that they were short a keyboard player for a song she was working on. Calls went out, and through her growing group of musician friends, she found that a player named Ben Margulies was available. Ben arrived at the studio, and as it turned out, he was not much of a keyboard player. But he survived the session, and during the course of casual conversation, Mariah found out that they had a lot in common. Yes, at age twenty-four, he was much older than the seventeen-year-old singer. But the age difference was easily overcome by a similar nature and creative passions. Mariah and Ben kept in touch and eventually decided to try writing together. As luck would have it, Ben's father had long ago given his son permission to set up a studio in a back room of his Manhattan cabinet factory. It was there that Ben and Mariah set about creating music together. The first song from this collaboration was the Motown-flavored "Here We Go Round Again." The songwriting chemistry was definitely there, Ben told the *New York Times*. "Mariah had the ability to just hear things in the air and to start developing songs out of them. Often, I would sit down and start playing something and from the feel of the chord, she would start singing melody lines and come up with a concept."

Mariah Carey's senior year at Harborfields High School was a busy one. The songwriting partnership with Ben Margulies was developing at a lightning pace, and the result was a number of quality songs. At this point, school was almost an afterthought for Mariah, but she kept her promise to her mother and attended just enough and did just well enough to get her diploma. She was already making plans to go to New York, be discovered, and become a big star. To the teachers and administrators who had spent four years trying to convince Mariah that dreams of singing stardom were little more than fantasy, an unreachable pipe dream, Mariah's future looked dark as they counted down the days to the graduation of the class of 1987. More than one teacher let Mariah know that if she ever needed any help, she should contact them.

The bond between Mariah and her mother had grown even stronger during the youngster's teen years as Patricia shared in her daughter's every musical step forward. Consequently, Mariah began to feel pangs of guilt at the prospect of running off to the big city and leaving her mother alone. Those feelings were salved shortly before graduation when her mother, after years of sacrificing a personal life to support her family, fell in love and married Joseph Vian.

In a sense, the marriage made it easier for Mariah to leave. Now she did not have to feel guilt, and she liked the idea that her mother had finally met a man who, as far as she could see, really cared for her. She could now focus totally on what she wanted to do, which was to go out into the world and make her own career and life — to follow her star. A week after her high-school graduation ceremony, Mariah Carey packed up her bare essentials and prepared to begin a new life. Next stop, New York.

CHAPTER THREE

In the City

Winter in New York just sort of sneaks up on you. The summer breezes turn steadily harsher and colder. Short sleeves and short skirts are slowly but surely replaced by long pants and heavy coats. Night falls sooner, and so does the snow. It is a winter wonderland — one that can be a little rough around the edges.

Mariah arrived in the Big Apple on the cusp of the change of the seasons. She had been to New York often enough to be familiar with the energy that seemed to rise up out of the ground and envelope the city. But now, she was looking at it through different eyes, eyes filled with expectation and anticipation. Mariah was excited at the prospect of changing her life, excited at the idea of New York now being her home. She was also apprehensive at the idea that for the first time, she was completely on her own. "It was wonderful and horrible at the same time," she recalled of her arrival in the city in an interview with *Veronica* magazine. "For the first time, I was on my own feet." Mariah was the dues-paying stereotype as she set out to make her fortune in New York City. She had one pair of worn shoes, no money, no connections, but a lot of confidence. And most importantly, she had a burning desire to make it on her own. Patricia's parting words to Mariah were that if she needed anything, just call. But she was too proud. "I could have asked people for money," she said, "but I felt I had to go with the feeling that got me there, and that was that I had to make it on my own."

Mariah scanned the want ads and soon found herself sharing a dive of an apartment with two other struggling performers. The apartment, in a rather seedy part of the city, was barely big enough for the other two and so, as last in, Mariah had to settle for sleeping on a mattress on the living room floor. Her first few months in New York were totally dedicated to the fine art of survival. None of the roommates had any money. They did not hold full-time jobs, and it was a constant struggle just to get the rent together every month. Food, as Mariah has painfully recalled, became almost an afterthought. A box of macaroni and cheese was the staple food item, and that typically had to last the three roommates a week. For several months, things were so dire that Mariah was subsisting on only one bagel and a bottle of iced tea a day, which she would bum from a sympathetic deli owner. Mariah had come to New York with basically one set of clothes: a short jacket, a pair of black stretch pants, and a pair of her mother's lace-up shoes. New clothes cost money, so Mariah wore what she had everywhere, no matter what the temperature was outside. "I had no money to buy a pair of shoes, and so I would walk around in the snow in shoes that had holes in them," she told a *Jet* reporter.

But there was more to Mariah's days and nights in New York than the struggles. At the time, there was a thriving music scene developing on the upper west side — a place where struggling musicians got together for informal jams and good times. Mariah recalled spending many nights just hanging out in a studio or an apartment watching her contemporaries, such as singer-songwriter Lenny Kravitz, as they set about trying to create a new musical universe. It was an electric atmosphere full of talent, promise, and hope, and Mariah felt comfortable in it. Despite her newcomer status, she felt a part of something real, creative, and musical.

Mariah's months in New York were punctuated by a series of what she considered dead-end jobs. They were the type of jobs that were relatively easy to come by, paid minimum wage or just tips, and seemed to be there for the sole purpose of allowing struggling actors, singers, and musicians an opportunity to pay the rent — but little else. Mariah would have preferred not to work and devote all her time to her musical career. She had never worked professionally at anything but music in her life and grudgingly went into formal employment. It came as no surprise that her attitude resulted in a whole lot of jobs that did not last very long. In no particular order, she held jobs as a coat-check girl, a hair sweeper in a beauty salon (which she quit after two days when the shop owner tried to get her to change her name to Echo), and, on many occasions, waitress in such New York landmarks as The Sports Bar and The Boathouse Cafe. As a waitress, Mariah was an absolute zero. By her own account, she would be rude to customers, mess up orders, and basically offer up the worst kind of service imaginable. She rarely got a good tip or any tip at all for that matter. Mariah told a *VH-1* interviewer that the reason she was such a bad waitress was that she could not keep her mind on her work. "I had this real bad attitude," she chuckled. "Why am I here? I want to be in the studio. I want to be singing. I want to be doing my thing." During breaks on the job, Mariah could usually be found slouched in a chair in some relatively quiet corner, scribbling out lyrics, hoping for inspiration amid the clatter of dishes and the shouts of customers. Her stint as the coat-check girl in a restaurant also allowed for some daydreaming, she recalled in an *US* magazine interview. "This place played videos, and I used to fantasize when I wrote that someday, I would come back and watch my own videos in the place. But the food wasn't that great, so I've never gone back."

Throughout her first year in New York, Mariah took great pains to be herself in every way, but she didn't discuss her secret longings in her everyday life. "I didn't tell anyone what I wanted to do," she confessed to *Q* magazine. "Every waitress in Manhattan was like 'Really, I'm an actress. Really, I'm a singer.' I just didn't want to be like that." It was a difficult time, but her salvation was her music. She'd get off a hellish late shift of waitressing, usually around midnight, and would meet up with her songwriting partner Ben Margulies at their cabinet-factory studio, and they would spend the remainder of the night creating magical songs. The pair had formed a cohesive unit, with Ben's music being the perfect conduit for Mariah's haunting lyrics.

Mariah and Ben had become the closest of friends and partners, but it was an unwritten rule between them that there would not be any romance. Not that Mariah had anything against men or the idea of falling in love, but she would not be distracted from her desire to make it. Quite naturally, that seemed to preclude any form of a love life. "I was so focused on getting a record deal and making an album that there was no room for anything else," she told the *Courier-Mail*. "People just don't understand that kind of drive and focus." It was a drive that would see Mariah regularly hand deliver her primitive demo tapes to the record company offices that lined the streets of New York. Mariah would seldom get any farther than the front desk where a receptionist would take her tape and promise to get it to the right person. Mariah was discouraged when the tapes would be either returned with a form rejection note or just disappear with no response at all. But mentally, she was made of tougher stuff, and so it did not take long for her to shake off the disappointment and move on.

Things began to pick up in 1988. Mariah's brother Morgan had also relocated to New York where he was working as a doorman at a local hot spot. Through his connections, he was able to get the club owner to book his sister for a series of performances on slow nights. Mariah was thrilled and frightened at the same time. While growing up, she began to struggle with her insecurities when it came to performing in public, and had not done it since grade school. By the time she had moved to New York, she had developed a full-blown phobia about being onstage. However, she finally decided to bite the bullet and try performing live in front of an audience of strangers. First and foremost, it would help her get over her fears. Second — and here was where the fantasy came in — you never knew who would be in the audience. It might be somebody who could change her life. By all accounts, during those shows, she was very nervous and had a hard time hiding it. Mariah readily admits that she was less than a dynamic performer in those early days. Nevertheless, those who saw her did come away impressed with the power of her vocals and the maturity of her songs. And things began to happen. The good word of mouth from those live performances, along with Ben's contacts began to widen Mariah's musical circle. A friend of Morgan's who had some experience offered to manage her. Musicians who had drifted in and out of her demo sessions with Ben began to talk her up, and she started getting a scattering of demo and backup singing jobs. Mariah gloried in the idea that she was moving in professional music circles and felt she was moving steadily up the ladder. It was just not far enough up so that she could escape the grind of waitressing.

One night, after a particularly miserable shift, Mariah was talking to a drummer who had been playing for a rhythm-and-blues singer named Brenda K. Starr. The musician told Mariah that one of Starr's backup singers had recently quit and that Starr was looking for a replacement. Mariah was reluctant at first, especially when she found out that Starr, despite being under contract to Epic Records, had not yet recorded an album and had so little money that she could not afford to keep her musicians and singers on more than a part-time basis. But her musician friend persisted and finally brought her around when he told her that it beat waitressing — anything would, she had to agree. So, on the appointed date, Mariah went to a small studio where Brenda K. Starr was holding auditions. There was an instant chemistry between the two, which probably accounts for the fact that they are still close, although Mariah went on to be a superstar and Brenda was only moderately successful. Starr was an easy and quite naturally friendly woman who had a mothering instinct, but that would not have made a bit of difference if Mariah had not blown her away during the audition with the strength and diversity of her voice. Mariah Carey aced the audition and was now in the big time — sort of.

The reality was that while Mariah did perform with Starr in a number of live shows, Brenda was two full years away from recording her first album, and so the money was not much better than what Mariah was pulling down as a waitress. But there was the experience of performing live in better situations, and that was something money could not buy. Brenda K. Starr was a rarity in the often cutthroat world of popular music. She was genuine, especially when it came to her dealings with Mariah. The singer was openly worried that Mariah's clothes were literally falling off her back and would often express her concern that her favorite backup singer would get sick. And while the unwritten rule in music was that the star should never do anything to promote a talented underling, Brenda Starr would go out of her way to help get her protégé in front of the right people. Brenda took every opportunity to introduce Mariah to her music-industry contacts and was quick to hand out copies of Mariah's demo tape to anyone who expressed the slightest interest. "She helped me out a lot," said Mariah in a 1991 *Ebony* interview. "She was always saying, 'Here's my friend Mariah. Here's her tape. She sings. She writes.'"

Late in the fall of 1988, Mariah received fantastic news. Her demo had found its way to the offices of Warner Bros. Records. The company was knocked out by her songs and that oh-so-smooth voice. They immediately offered her a solo recording contract with a $300,000 advance, and they selected one of her songs to be included on a sound-track album for an upcoming motion picture. Her manager warned her that the deal would take some time to finalize but that did not stop Mariah from literally dancing on air as a result of this big break. So, her persistence had paid off. Less than a year after coming to New York, she was about to be signed to a major label. Stardom was right around the corner.

But while the prospect of having her dreams come true loomed on the horizon, the reality was that she still had to pay the rent. Fortunately, her growing popularity and the status of being with Brenda had led to a fairly full schedule of demo sessions as well as the occasional backup gig with Brenda. Mariah was overworked, running on fumes, and she wanted nothing more than a bed and eight uninterrupted hours of sleep. Which was why all she could do was groan one Friday night in November 1988 when Brenda pestered her to tag along to a party being held for the brand-new record label WTG Records. Brenda insisted that it would be a good place to make connections, that she needed to have a little fun, and that there would be free food. She was certainly tempted by the thought of free food, but tried to beg off with the excuse that she was tired, hated socializing, and had nothing to wear. Brenda insisted that she would loan her some clothes and instantly produced a mini skirt, a cheerleader coat, and a pair of sneakers. Mariah could not help but laugh at the bizarre ensemble, but once she stopped laughing, she agreed to go to the party.

It was the typical music-biz get-together. Lots of shoptalk and lots of men a lot older than Mariah was. She made the most of the food, but, true to her antisocial ways, she stayed pretty much to herself, huddling close to Brenda throughout the evening. Brenda was the perfect guide, pointing out important, potentially influential record-company people and explaining to her that getting her tape into the hands of WTG Records president Jerry Greenberg would be a good idea despite the fact that she was close to a deal with Warner Bros. Late in the evening, Brenda pointed out Greenberg across the room. As Mariah looked, she noticed that the man Greenberg was talking to looked back. And that was the first time Mariah Carey locked eyes with Tommy Mottola. "Tommy was just looking at me," recalled Mariah in a *Courier-Mail* article. "I was like this eighteen-year-old-girl in an Avirex jacket, in a miniskirt and sneakers. I think he probably had a little Lolita thing going on."

As the evening began to wind down, Brenda kept insisting that Mariah approach Greenberg with her tape, but she continued to hang back. Finally, Brenda took the tape from Mariah's bag and said she would do the honors. In a 1996 *Vibe* interview, Mariah recalled what happened next: "Brenda went over and started to hand the tape to Jerry Greenberg, but Tommy put out his hand, grabbed the tape, and snatched it away." Tommy Mottola did indeed take note of the striking and innocent-looking Mariah who was

Mariah with Tommy Mottola

more than twenty years his junior. But while the first thing he had noticed was her beauty, his instincts, borne of more than thirty years in the record biz as a performer, manager, and now the new president of Sony Records, made him take that tape. Something had told him there might just be some talent behind this young woman's exotic good looks. Mottola left the party a few minutes later, tape in hand. Brenda was excited that the head of Sony Records had taken the tape with him, but Mariah, burned by almost a year's worth of rejection, was a little more cautious about getting her hopes up. And, indeed, why should she with the Warner Bros. deal all but assured? As she and Brenda were leaving the party, Mariah realized that the tape did not have her phone number on it.

During his limo ride home from the party, Mottola took the tape out and popped it into a cassette player. Mariah's voice and the sincerity of her lyrics literally pinned him back in his seat. Two songs into the four-song tape, Mottola yelled up at his driver to turn around and return to the party. Mottola looked high and low for Mariah but could not find her. She and Brenda had already left. The record-company president spent a long weekend contemplating the irony of finding a true star only to lose her just like Cinderella. But he remembered that she had arrived with Brenda, and that was a good place to start. So, on Monday morning, he rang up Brenda's management company and tracked down Mariah's telephone number. "Hi. This is Tommy Mottola. Call me back." This was the message that greeted Mariah when she came home from work that day. Once she got over her shock, she returned his call. She recalled being scared to death as she spoke to Mottola for the first time. Mottola was more sub-dued but equally excited at the prospects for Mariah. He simply said, "I think we can make hit records."

As with most Hollywood stories, what happened next has taken on almost legendary proportions and is open to conjecture. The popular myth is that that same afternoon, Mariah, accompanied by her mother Patricia, entered the office of the Sony Records president and listened as Mottola praised her talents and promised a bright future. However, there was one stumbling block. Warner Bros. was still interested in Mariah, and would be even more so when they discovered that she was being aggressively courted by Mottola and Sony. A minor bidding war ensued that was ulti-mately won by Sony. But in recent years, an alternative and just-as-viable version of the story has surfaced. According to nameless former record-company employees cited in a *Vanity Fair* article on Mottola, Mariah showed up at Tommy Mottola's office with Ben Margulies. Tommy immediately concluded that Ben was Mariah's boyfriend and took an instant dislike to him. According to the *Vanity Fair* sources, Mottola decided that he would do everything possible to shove Ben out of the picture. As for that bidding war, the *Vanity Fair* article reported that once Mottola heard about the Warner Bros. offer, he upped the ante to $350,000, $50,000 more than the Warner advance. That sealed the deal.

Whatever the truth, in December 1988, Mariah Carey signed on the bottom line with Sony Records. The glass slipper of fame was a perfect fit.

CHAPTER FOUR

First Time's the Charm

"When I heard and saw Mariah, there was absolutely no doubt that she was, in every way, destined for stardom," Tommy Mottola explained in a *New York Times* interview. Tommy knew talent, but he was also a clear-headed businessman, and that side of him saw a well-defined bottom line. Mariah was too caught up in the fantasy and excitement of the moment to worry about the business implications of her career. In the days following the official signing with Sony, she was busy calling family and friends with the good news, being introduced to myriad new people in the Sony building and trying to match up names and faces, laying out money for a decent wardrobe, and basically reveling in the fact that she was now a full-fledged recording artist. She was so wrapped up in the moment that she was completely unaware of the whispers in the Sony hallways in the days after she signed with the new company. Mariah Carey was more than just new talent; she was being counted on to fill a hole in Sony's music catalog. The label, with its Columbia lineage, included such successful acts as George Michael and Michael Bolton, but there was a bit of a hole in the area of contemporary, middle-of-the-road pop music. Pop divas who could deliver big, heartfelt ballads were all the rage in the late eighties, and, for all its diversity, Sony had nobody who could compare with the reigning queens of the genre — Whitney Houston, Janet Jackson, and Madonna. And so, while Mottola liked Mariah's basic approach, the ink had barely dried on her contract when the record-company head started bringing in people who would help shape her sound into a viable commercial product.

Tommy's moves immediately put him in conflict with Mariah and long-time writing partner Ben Margulies. The songs that had landed Mariah the contract had essentially been written by the two of them over a three-year-period. They knew the heart and soul of the songs better than anybody else and just naturally assumed that they would coproduce the album themselves. And so, Mariah was more than a bit concerned when she found herself, mere days after signing with Sony, being introduced to a list of superstar producer-songwriters that included Ric Wake, Rhett Lawrence, and Narada Michael Walden. They had been involved with some pretty impressive names, including Michael Jackson, Earth, Wind & Fire, and Smokey Robinson. But she did not know these producers. She did not know what they were like or how they worked, and she was troubled. Mariah was instantly put off by the idea of working with a big-name producer. She was afraid, perhaps rightly so, that her songs and her sound would be homogenized by people unfamiliar with her. She didn't want her music turned into just another faceless and soulless album. While also concerned at the prospect of losing creative control, Ben seemed to take the slight a lot better than Mariah. He was philosophical about being eliminated from the mix, seeing it as something that inevitably occurs in the music business. He encouraged Mariah and praised the talents of the chosen producers. After all, if nothing else, they could still write some great songs together. And they proved it shortly after Mariah signed her contract when they created the song "Vision of Love."

The first perk of stardom — more money than Mariah had seen in her entire life — began to come her way. It would have been easy to go hog wild after so many years of living on tight budgets, but Mariah, as befitting her upbringing and simple lifestyle, was cautious. She rented a one-bedroom apartment on New York's upper east side, splurged on a new Mustang convertible, and bought clothes — lots of clothes. Watching Mariah spend money in those halcyon days was amusing in a way. She could have just about anything she wanted but agonized over the simplest purchases as if one false move might make all of it go away. Not that she would have time to go anywhere to show off her new car and clothes. Almost immediately, Mariah was plunged into the long and challenging process of recording her first album, *Mariah Carey*.

Mariah had no idea what the approach to her debut disc would be. Her attitude was that she would just go into the studio and sing, keeping the arrangements fairly simple. The producers were knocked out by Mariah's multioctave vocals, and they liked much of what she and Ben had written. In fact, as it turned out, there would be the inevitable restructuring of arrangements and changes of tempos in the songwriting stages, but, when the dust settled, six of the album's ten songs and three of the four number one hits would be Mariah-Ben compositions. Mariah was a bit unsure about what it would be like to write with these three producers, and in the early days of her respective sessions, she was concerned that her ideas would be brushed aside in favor of theirs. But to a person, all were respectful of Mariah's talents and ideas. And after getting over the initial shock of writing with someone besides Ben, Mariah found collaborating with others to be a challenging and often exhilarating experience. With producer Wake, Mariah wrote four songs of which "There's Got to Be a Way" would make it onto the album. Her writing sessions with Walden produced the ballad "I Don't Wanna Cry," which went on to be a number one hit. Rhett Lawrence was instrumental in shaping "Vision of Love" into a more heartfelt, torchy song than Mariah and Ben had originally intended.

Mariah racked up the frequent-flyer miles making her debut album in New York, Los Angeles, and San Rafael, California. She found recording an often dizzying, high-speed experience — the endless takes, the accidents that became divine inspiration, the long days and nights that stretched into the early morning. This was all new to her, and despite the pressure on her to succeed, she thrived on it. Mariah was the perfect student; she was never a puppet, but she was always willing to compromise when a better idea was offered up. Even at times when her presence was not necessary in the studio, she would be there soaking up the vibe as she watched an all-star lineup of session musicians lay down the tracks and the engineers manipulate her sound into something glossy and seamless. There were moments during the recording sessions when Mariah felt that the arrangements were overly theatrical and a bit old-fashioned, and she would question the producers about it. They would patiently explain why they felt something worked and would tweak something to Mariah's taste if she insisted. Mariah sensed, perhaps naively, that she was in her element, part of the whole process, and that she had finally arrived.

Long before *Mariah Carey* had even reached the final mixdown stage, Sony Records had designated the twenty-year-old singer as a "priority artist," corporatespeak for "pull out all the stops to make her a star." Mariah was now officially the center of a money-is-no-object publicity and marketing campaign designed to put this unknown singer's name on the lips of radio programmers, record retailers, and all the important cogs that go into making a hit record. Once again, it was Tommy Mottola who was very much the Svengali, heading up meetings with publicity and promotions departments and investing a lot more personal attention than most first-time artists received from the head man.

"We had numerous meetings about Mariah way in advance of the record's release," said Jane Berk, former director of marketing for Columbia Records, in a *New York Times* feature. "It was all very strategically planned." The first step was to have Mariah perform live at a spring 1990 Los Angeles convention of the National Association of Recording Merchandisers, an annual gathering of the heads of the biggest record-store chains in the country. But Mariah was not thrilled that this was happening in the midst of struggling to finish up the album. She had long ago stopped thinking of herself as anything more than a mediocre live performer, one prone to onstage nerves and preshow panics. She had been able to overcome those fears in her early performances and at a private showcase for CBS record executives and sales representatives a few weeks earlier. Mariah could not get over the fact that a lot was riding on her small shoulders, and that it was up to her to impress a roomful of jaded, high-powered strangers. But Mariah was still at the stage where she was grateful for the opportunity Sony had given her and felt compelled to agree to virtually every suggestion. Mariah's performance was a mixed bag according to those who witnessed it. She arrived onstage stiff with obvious nervousness, but once she began to sing, the record-store execs were easily won over by her soaring, multioctave voice. "Her performance was good but not incredible," recalled record-store-chain executive Howard Applebaum. "But the energy level in that room was astounding."

Mariah was not through performing live. Rather than just send retailer tapes to radio programmers and regional sales people, Mottola decided to send Mariah on an ambitious and quite expensive, nine-city promotional tour, and at each stop, she would perform a brief live set. After her initial jitters at the Los Angeles promotional event, Mariah was feeling a little more comfortable performing live. The result was a lot of positive feedback and word of mouth that resulted in increased orders for *Mariah Carey* from the record chains and promises of early airplay from the radio programmers.

In the weeks leading up to the June 1990 release of her debut album, Mariah was spending almost all her time surrounded by Sony executives and producers. But she did find some spare moments to hang out with Ben Margulies and, as usually happened, their casual chats turned to a musical lick, a fragment of a lyric, and, before they knew it, the two had created the song "Love Takes Time." Since her debut disc was all but wrapped up and on its way to pressing, the pair assumed they would keep this song for her follow-up album. However, Tommy Mottola had other ideas. As soon as he heard the song, he knew it was a number one record and that it had to be on the album. Mariah was literally running on empty after months in the recording studio and the hectic promotional campaign. She needed a break in the worst way, and she would get it — after she recorded "Love Takes Time." In a three-day marathon that covered both coasts, the song was arranged, recorded, and mastered with the aid of a little-known producer named Walter Afanasieff. The first few hundred copies of *Mariah Carey* rattled off the presses and were immediately collector items — the song "Love Takes Time" was on the album, but it was not listed on the album sleeve. But that problem was quickly rectified, and the consensus was that the song would be a smash hit.

The brain trust at Sony had decided that "Vision of Love" would be the first single off the album. This being the era of MTV, a video was immediately ordered and shot. Mariah was surprisingly comfortable with the video process and eased through the endless takes and hours it took to bring "Visions of Love" to life. But when Mariah and the studio executives saw it, they were not happy. Part and parcel of the packaging of Mariah Carey was to project a certain image, and they all agreed that the first video did not work in bringing Mariah's image of a young, sultry diva to life. And so in an unheard of situation for a new artist, Sony reshot the whole thing at considerable added expense. This new video got their full approval. But this latest bit of preferential treatment only succeeded in fueling the rumors that were already flying about the true nature of the relationship between Mariah and Tommy Mottola. Word on the street was that Mottola's once rock-solid nineteen-year marriage was suddenly in trouble and that the cause was Mottola's alleged, quickly blooming romantic relationship with Mariah. Whether the rumors were true or not, there was a lot of evidence pointing to the fact that their relationship was more than professional. From the moment she signed with Sony, it seemed that

Mariah was spending every waking hour with Mottola or under his direct influence, with the obvious preferential treatment accorded Mariah that few artists had ever received from the label. Adding fuel to the fire was the gossip that Mariah was involved romantically with somebody who she refused to name. Mariah was taken aback by her first brush with rumor and sensationalism. When questions of a personal nature were asked in early press interviews, she simply refused to answer them, but not knowing how to play the media game, she would hint at a relationship, stating that she did have a boyfriend but would not go into any further details.

The reality was that by the time Mariah had completed her first album, she and Tommy were very much in love. In later years, Mariah would often say that "It just sort of happened, and that we had a lot in common." But in a sense, Mariah and Tommy coming together was an age-old Hollywood story. A young, somewhat naive girl and a much older, driven man are thrown together. Mottola's love for and knowledge of music combined with his nonstuffy attitude toward the business probably also had a lot to do with their developing friendship and relationship. Whatever the reason, sparks had begun to fly in a matter of weeks. "Our relationship was kind of a different thing," said Mariah in a 1996 *Vibe* magazine interview. "There definitely was some kind of chemistry going on that was really intense." However, there were innumerable reasons why the pair could not go public with their relationship. Unknown to the public, Tommy was in the middle of a legal separation that was already heading for an ugly divorce. His professional treatment of Mariah would surely lead to conflict-of-interest charges if their relationship became known. Finally, Mariah being tarred as "the other woman" was not the kind of publicity most newcomers race toward. For all these reasons, Mariah and Tommy were the models of discretion during the early months of their relationship.

In the meantime, the *Mariah Carey* publicity train kept on rolling. Early in June, Mariah did guest shots on top-rated late-night shows *The Arsenio Hall Show* and *The Tonight Show Starring Johnny Carson*. Strings were also pulled to allow Mariah to sing "America the Beautiful" at game one of the NBA basketball finals. The groundwork for Mariah's debut had been laid with the precision of a military campaign and the advancing army was successful. The feedback had been tremendous, but inside the halls of Sony and especially in the office of Tommy Mottola, fingers were crossed. New artists are a risky proposition at any time, but as the bean counters added up the expenses in *Mariah Carey*'s ledger ($800,000 to produce the album, $500,000 for the video, and a cool million for promotion), a lot of worst-case scenarios were being played out. For Mariah, failure would be a disappointment, but for Sony, it could spell disaster in a world in which perception is everything.

The year 1990 was a maddeningly inconsistent time in popular music. Alternate-grunge rock and the stylistically smooth sounds of Whitney Houston and other divas were fighting for ever-decreasing radio playlist slots with the last gasps of heavy metal and an emerging, vital second British Invasion. The competition was so fierce that radio programmers were likely to dismiss quickly anything that they considered a weak debut effort. So a strong first single was all important. If "Vision of Love" was not an immediate hit, getting a second single by Mariah Carey on the air was going to be extra tough. Fortunately, "Vision of Love" began pouring out of radios in late May 1990, and by June 2, it entered *Billboard*'s Top 100 list at number seventy-three. The song was an instant smash, moving steadily up the charts and priming audiences for the June 30 release of the debut album *Mariah Carey*. The album debuted at number eighty on the *Billboard* charts, pushing the rapid rise of "Vision of Love" to number one by August 4, a position it would occupy for four consecutive weeks. The album quickly followed suit and would eventually enjoy a twenty-two-week run at number one. *Mariah Carey* quickly went platinum (one million copies sold) and, in quick order, cracked six million.

There was a good reason for the album's success. Most new artists tend to rely on one tone, one musical mood to carry the day. But Mariah's debut was a mix of styles and tempos demonstrating her versatility and the range of her talent. "Vision of Love" proved to be the perfect radio song. Mildly dramatic in an agreeable pop way, it provided a particularly strong statement for Mariah's multioctave range. "There's Got to Be a Way" was a showcase of Mariah's songwriting skills as well as her sense of society's ills. Again, her voice was the song's guiding light, but, like much of Mariah's songs that would come in later years, there was much in "There's Got to Be a Way" that was subtle, particularly in the song's arrangement.

Two particularly contrasting pieces on the album were "Someday" and "Vanishing." The former was a lighter-than-air dance tune that played studio technology off against a soaring Mariah vocal. Written with Ben

Margulies, the song also hit number one in 1991. The latter song, a simply constructed ballad, blended together Mariah's vocals and a simple piano arrangement for maximum effect. The remainder of *Mariah Carey* continued to strike that delicate balance. While Mariah was barely out of her teens, her musical vocabulary was nothing if not adult in nature, and her appeal reached well beyond her own age group.

Mariah was a bit surprised at the success of her debut album, but her naiveté was keeping her ego in check. She would often exclaim that the big thing in her life was to hear her songs coming out of the radio, and that wish was quickly fulfilled. Also, at the time that *Mariah Carey* was burning up the charts, the young singer was already back in the studio working on songs for her next album. This desire to keep forging ahead stemmed from Mariah's childhood when continuous moving and a basic lack of security were her constant companions. On a very conscious level, Mariah felt that the only way to keep the rug from suddenly being pulled out from under her dream was to keep creating. Not too surprisingly, the executives at Sony were thrilled at the idea. The careers of pop singers are notoriously short owing to the fickle nature of music buyers who are always on the lookout for the next big thing. And while Mariah, even at this early date, was already showing the kind of depth and staying power that translates into a long career, Sony was not going to say no to another album so soon after her debut.

With the across-the-board success of the album came the inevitable calls for Mariah to tour. Mottola had known early on that coaxing Mariah at this point onstage to sing could be difficult, and that a premature tour and less-than-favorable reviews might deal a damaging blow to the singer's fragile ego. So, he wisely turned down big money and offers of major venues from promoters. The Sony executive had been down this road before with artists who were great in the studio but less-than-dynamic in a live setting. And he had seen what the press could do once they got hold of the idea that a performer had even the hint of stage fright. Besides, Mottola had already agreed to one live gig. In exchange for radio station KMEL being the first to put "Vision of Love" into its regular rotation, Mottola said that Mariah would perform at the outdoor concert Summer Jam, which was being sponsored by the radio station and held in Mountain View, California. Mariah reluctantly agreed. She still wasn't very comfortable with performing but felt she had to force herself to do it because it came with the territory. "Touring is hard for me because I'm not a ham," she once explained to *USA Today*. "You have to be dynamic and showy, and that's not second nature to me. I didn't get a chance to work my way up from the clubs, so performing is still pretty scary." At the Summer Jam concert, Mariah was her usual bundle of nerves moments before she stepped onstage. However, by the time the applause died down, she was in control and went on to deliver a powerful set, highlighted by her sweet, soulful voice and music that ran the gamut of taste from light dance to pure pop, and finally to her true strength — dramatic, powerful ballads like "Vision of Love."

The reviews of *Mariah Carey* were almost universal in their praise of her upper-register singing voice and remarkable songwriting skills, particularly for somebody so young. Even those reviewers who complained about the overly slick production and what they perceived as by-the-numbers arrangements pointed out that the album was, nonetheless, a promising debut. That "Vision of Love" was an immediate hit felt like a personal triumph more than a commercial one for Mariah. "That song represents everything in my life," she said in *Ebony*. "It is a song from the heart." Mariah was aware that the songs on *Mariah Carey* had come from a very personal place and that many of them reflected on the hard times growing up and her struggles for a sense of personal and professional freedom. "A lot of the songs were written when I was kind of struggling," she explained in a *Chicago Tribune* article. "It was a harrowing emotional time in my life. They [the songs] weren't necessarily all about relationships, but they were about things happening in my life."

But what Mariah was not ready for was the viciousness of some of the reviewers who chose to dismiss her as another white girl trying to exploit black music for her own gain. These were reviews that totally dismissed the quality of her music and chose instead to make personal assumptions about the character of the performer. The barbs were particularly hurtful to Mariah for a couple of reasons. First, she was not white but biracial. Then, there was the fact that this was the kind of music she had grown up on and loved. Why, she reasoned, should she be penalized for that? The singer hammered these points home in subsequent interviews, and eventually the naysayers went away, but for Mariah, the charges just reinforced the fact that she was, indeed, different. No amount of success was going to change that.

Mariah wins 1991 Grammys for Best Pop Vocal Performance
and Best New Artist

Mariah made another television appearance in October as the main musical guest on *Saturday Night Live*, long known as a groundbreaker for hot new acts. While her album remained atop the *Billboard* charts, her first single was beginning to fall. Without missing a beat, her second single "Love Takes Time" was released and by November, had followed "Vision of Love" to the number one spot. A hit record generally needs a video, and although Mariah did not completely understand the need for a video as a tool to sell music, she went along and found the process that resulted in the romantically themed video for "Love Takes Time" to be a lot of fun.

The last few months of 1990 were a blur of good vibes. Mariah could not go anywhere without hearing her music on the radio. She was being recognized on the street and was thrilled the first time she was asked for her autograph. The singer was being besieged with interview requests, and she was attending all the right parties and, increasingly in the public eye, on the arm of Tommy Mottola. Stardom was proving to be a heady elixir for Mariah Carey. Nevertheless, Mariah was instinctively cautious lest she become engulfed by the hype. When she would hear herself described as "the franchise" by suits from Sony Records, she would wrinkle her nose in distaste. With stardom literally at her feet, she was suddenly uncomfortable with it. "I don't let this stuff go to my head," she once said. "I don't want to be a big star. I want to be respected as an artist." But stardom is exactly what she was getting. Mariah was finding herself on the most influential critic's Top-Ten lists for the year in a number of categories including best new artist and best album. The icing on the cake came when the prestigious Grammy Awards were announced, and Mariah found herself nominated in five different categories: Best Pop Vocal Performance — Female, Best New Artist, Album of the Year, Song of the Year, and Best Album. Making the dream complete was the invitation to perform her signature song "Vision of Love" in front of a Grammy audience that would number in excess of twenty million worldwide.

Although Mariah was very familiar with the streets of New York, on the night of the Grammy Awards, as her limo whisked her and Tommy toward Radio City Music Hall and the award ceremony, she was seeing the city and her world in a different light. Dressed in a short black dress, she was very much Cinderella on her way to the ball. She was in love with a life that was continuing, at every turn, to be a fairy tale. Mariah was all smiles as she walked down the red carpet and the photographers yelled for her attention. There were also screams from the bleachers where the growing legion of diehard fans had braved the cold for a glimpse of their hero. Mariah responded with a smile and a wave. That night, despite the usual bout of nerves, Mariah gave an emotion-filled performance of "Vision of Love" before returning to her seat to nervously wait out the moment she had been waiting for. The realist in Mariah felt that just being nominated was enough of a validation, but the little girl in her hoped that some of the top honors would be hers. Her hopes were rewarded later in the evening when she returned to the stage to accept two statues: the Grammys for Best New Artist and Best Pop Vocal Performance — Female.

After the ceremony, Mariah attended a series of celebrations where she mingled with some of the biggest names in music, and she basked in their praise as both a powerful new talent and a superstar on the rise. But her Cinderella story would have a much different ending than the original fairy tale. When the clock struck midnight, she did not return to the role of struggling unknown. She remained a star — and she continued to party until dawn.

CHAPTER FIVE

Second
That Emotion

The accolades and kudos continued to pour in for Mariah. The hoopla surrounding her Grammy victories had barely died down when she was recognized by *Rolling Stone* magazine as Best New Female Singer in its annual readers' poll. One week later, she captured Best New Artist, Best New Single, and Best New Album honors at the annual Soul Train Awards. Mariah soaked up the recognition with no small amount of humility. Mariah, still very much the shy, insecure girl, was unsettled by the amount of media attention and hype she was receiving. In a sense, she felt that all the interest was being directed at another person she did not know. Mariah remembered all too well how she had felt growing up when her heroes were often picked apart in the media, and she was not happy at the prospect of the same thing happening to her. "I don't want to put myself in everyone's face and make them sick of me at this early stage of my career," she once said. "I want to be around for a while." That was one reason why Mariah cut back considerably on the amount of media interviews she did in the wake of *Mariah Carey*'s release. Furthermore, she felt talked out, and there really was not that much new that she could say. It was an instinctive need, in the face of all this attention, to retain a low profile. Her attitude was to let her music do the talking — and talk it did!

"Someday" was released as a single in early January 1991 and quickly became Mariah's third number-one hit off *Mariah Carey* within three months. At a time when Mariah should have been able to take time off to recharge her creative batteries, the reality of the music business as well as her own drive to keep going was forcing her to face another round of decisions. Once again, the question was raised about following up the hit album with a huge tour. But Mariah was still not confident enough in her performing skills to take that step, and the Sony brain trust felt that with the success of her debut album, a tour was not essential at this point. Moreover, the reality was that even a small tour could delay a follow-up album. However, there was more than avoiding touring fueling Mariah's inclination to return to the studio as soon as possible. Mariah's mind was constantly filled with music, and by the time *Mariah Carey* hit the streets, the singer-songwriter was already working overtime on ideas she felt would be her next musical step. And she planned to make it a step away from the concept of her successful debut album.

Despite its overwhelming success, Mariah was not completely satisfied with her first album. Lyrically and musically, she felt *Mariah Carey* was her best effort at that moment in time, but she continued to chaff at what she considered the overly extravagant arrangements and orchestration which she felt often blunted the emotional intent of the songs. She felt the blame was hers. She had been too much of a babe in the woods to put her foot down on certain creative issues during the making of *Mariah Carey*, but she vowed that would not be the case next time. Mariah envisioned her next album as homage to the Motown sound she grew up with. She wanted the album to duplicate the experience she had had hearing the songs of that era emanating from the radio or off a spinning piece of vinyl. Yes, there would be the expected balance of ballads and dance numbers but, she reasoned, this time the songs would not be as overly produced and slick as they had been on *Mariah Carey*. This time, she wanted to come across as more soulful. "I felt I should put out a new album soon because I was growing so much from the last album," Mariah told the *New York Times*.

Mariah instinctively turned to her muse Ben Margulies. Unfortunately, much had changed in their relationship since the release of *Mariah Carey*. She now found that his back was turned to her. Not long after Mariah and Ben had teamed up, Mariah had impulsively signed a contract with Ben that would entitle him to half the proceeds she made from any recordings involving his material. With the success of *Mariah Carey*, he was already making substantial money off the songwriting royalties. But now, Ben was uncharacteristically pushing for more — what he felt was his contractually. The conversations between the writing partners were not angry, but they were strained at times. Ben quietly pointed out that she had agreed to the terms of the contract, and that he had not twisted her arm. Mariah did not deny she had willingly signed the contract but felt Ben was asking for too much and tried to persuade him to not press the issue. He refused. At that point, Sony's lawyers stepped in, and after a long and often bitter court battle that dragged on for over a year, both sides reportedly agreed that Ben would receive ten percent of Mariah's earnings over the next ten years. Mariah would look back on the falling out with Ben as a painful learning experience. "Be careful what you sign," she said in a *Q* magazine interview. "I heard that a thousand times. But when you're struggling, you still do it. I blindly signed." In the aftermath of the court battle, Ben would discuss the situation diplomatically, putting the lion's share of the blame on the record label and saying that he hoped Mariah and he could work together again in the future. The reality was that a five-year friendship and creative partner-ship that had produced some wonderful music had been destroyed. The two never worked together again and, in fact, had no contact whatsoever.

Sony had agreed in principle to Mariah's plans for her follow-up album. But the nuts-and-bolts blueprint for her second album, *Emotions*, was once again laid out by the record company in much the same manner as it was for *Mariah Carey*. Again, it involved a number of songwriters and produc-ers. For the more up-tempo songs, the producing–writing team of David Cole and Robert Clivillés were chosen. The pair made their name with club and dance music groups, producing hits such as C&C Music Factory's "Gonna Make You Sweat." Despite his ease with arrangements and his proven ability to work under pressure, Walter Afanasieff was considered a surprise choice to produce the ballads. Sony, with their collective eye always on the bottom line, had wanted somebody with what they consid-ered more commercial songwriting ability and a more substantial résumé. But Mariah, who had a good experience working with Walter on "Love Takes Time" and on demos of new songs at the end of 1990, insisted that Afanasieff had to be on board. And, for once, Sony blinked, and Walter became part of the team. But the company would not budge on the notion that each song had to be presented to the studio executives for their thumbs up or thumbs down. This process was fairly common in the recording indus-try, but Mariah would grow to resent the fact that people who knew only how to make money should pass judgment on her creative efforts.

The last vestiges of spring were slipping over into summer. The fourth and final single off the persistent bestseller *Mariah Carey*, "I Don't Wanna Cry," had just debuted at number fifty and, within two weeks, hit number one. But Mariah barely noticed since she was already ensconced in another intense period of bicoastal writing and recording of new songs. As in the past, the dance tunes were being recorded in New York, while the ballads, with Walter Afanasieff at the controls, were done in California. And much like the recording of *Mariah Carey*, the singer found working with multiple producers to be a widely divergent experience. With Clivillés and Cole, the formula was simple. They would bring in tapes of different rhythms, Mariah would pick what she liked, and the lyrics would flow from there. Mariah found Clivillés and Cole to be easygoing and hip producers whose train of thought was very much in sync with hers. With Afanasieff, the creative give-and-take was more gentle and quietly spontaneous, with ideas on everything from arrangement to lyrics to production gone over with a fine-tooth comb. It was not the same as having Ben around, but it was pretty close.

In all cases, however, Mariah, secure and confident in her own talents with the success of *Mariah Carey*, was very much involved with every element of the album's creation. And, unlike her experience on the debut album, she was no longer shy about voicing her likes and dislikes and sticking to her guns. "I didn't want this album to be somebody else's vision of me," she said in *USA Today*. "This time, I really collaborated. There's more of me on this album, and I let myself go a lot more." But being taken seriously was still an uphill battle. In the back of everybody's mind was the fact that Mariah was still considered a studio creation whose true talents lay with her producers. The reality was that on *Emotions*, the producers did listen and found much to their liking in the singer's suggestions and ideas.

Easily the biggest surprise to come out of the *Emotions* sessions was the telephone call Mariah received one day from legendary singer-songwriter Carole King, who suggested that she might consider doing a cover of the King-penned song "Natural Woman," which had been a monster hit for Aretha Franklin. That song would have definitely been in the loop for Mariah's trip back to Motown. But she hesitated. "I didn't want to," said Mariah in a *New York* magazine interview, "because Aretha's one of my idols, and I felt what she did with the song was an untouchable performance." However, King was so impressed with Mariah's talent and integrity that she did not give up that easily. King flew from her home in Idaho to

New York for a one-day writing session with Mariah in hopes that maybe they could hammer out something she could use. The result was a literal meeting of minds across the generations in which Mariah's budding talents traded ideas with King's wealth of experience in the art of songwriting. The day's collaboration produced the song "If It's Over." It did not become a hit, but there was satisfaction in the collaboration between the two women.

It was during the recording of *Emotions* that Tommy Mottola's divorce became final, and he and Mariah were at last free to go public with their romance. On a regular basis, gossip columns began to report on the couple, hand in hand at various showbiz functions, and more than one person would recall seeing Tommy and Mariah necking in a back booth of one of their favorite New York pubs.

Mariah was in a good place personally and professionally, but as the August 31 release date of *Emotions* neared, Sony executives once again had their fingers crossed, while critics were sharpening their pencils. Mariah had not gone through *Mariah Carey* completely unscathed. More than one reviewer dismissed her as little more than a thinly disguised Whitney Houston clone. Others had intimated that her music was bland and inoffensive, typical of the passive, forgettable songs being played on Top Forty radio. But she had weathered those criticisms and accusations and no longer feared the critics. On the other hand, Sony bosses did. Specifically, they were afraid that all the hype and media coverage might backfire and make Mariah into yet another one-hit wonder unless *Emotions* was truly a masterpiece.

The album would turn out to be a step forward, but true to her promise, it was also an enticing step back. The arrangements, as befitting a Motown homage, were sparer and simpler than Walter Afanasieff's admittedly overly orchestrated work on much of *Mariah Carey*. Just about everything on *Emotions* — with its deep soul and flecks of gospel dancing the perimeters of most of the songs — was streaked with an older style. "If It's Over" turned out to be truest to Mariah's retro approach. That song screamed sixties soul and vocally, Mariah was more than a mere echo of the greats of years gone by. She proved that under the right circumstances, she could definitely stand with them. The quiet songs like "So Blessed" and "'Till the End of Time," and the melancholy in Mariah's voice on the jazz-heavy "The Wind" made these standouts in an album that was perhaps more experimental than some mainstream pop sensibilities might care for. *Emotions* would most certainly be a love-it-or-hate-it album. It was time to roll the dice.

The title single off the *Emotions* album made its debut on August 31, 1991 at number thirty-five on the *Billboard* charts. The album followed shortly, but there were immediate signs that Mariah's momentum might be slowing down. "Emotions" took six weeks to get to number one, and the album also moved slowly and eventually topped out at number four. The reasons for this sluggish but by no means unspectacular showing for *Emotions* were many. Sony had pulled back on the pre-release promotion for the album, preferring to let word of mouth and all the goodwill from Mariah's first album carry over. Reviews were decidedly mixed, many focusing on what critics considered the inconsistent quality of the songs. But like the previous disc, there was praise for her singing ability and the courageous decision to play in the influential field of Motown.

Mariah continued on the high road of success. Unfortunately, with success came attacks from those on the periphery of her life who wanted a piece of the growing pie. In a sense, her falling-out with Ben and the ensuing legal battles signaled that these types of situations would arise from time to time. But it hurt most when the deepest cut came from Mariah's immediate family. The marriage of Patricia Carey and Joseph Vian had been a rocky one from the beginning, and so nobody was too surprised when the couple separated in 1992 and began divorce proceedings. What was surprising was that Vian, with whom Mariah had always been cordial but not particularly close, filed a lawsuit against Mariah in New York's Federal District Court. To say the least, the charges made against the singer were unusual. According to published reports, Vian alleged that Mariah had made an oral commitment to him that would allow him to market singing Mariah Carey dolls. He also claimed to be entitled to financial reimbursement for his alleged contributions to the development of Mariah's professional career. He saved the most outlandish charge for last: Mariah had contributed to the breakup of his marriage to Patricia. Mariah vehemently denied all the charges but knew the only way to fight them was in court.

Not long after the case against her stepfather began to unfold, Mariah was once again blindsided. Songwriters Sharon Taber and Randy Gonzalez filed suit against Mariah, charging that the song "Can't Let Go" from the

Emotions album had deliberately lifted nine notes from their song "Right Before My Eyes," which they had copyrighted in 1990. The pair further charged that a tape of their song had been passed on to Mariah from one of her backup singers who happened to be a friend of Taber's. Once again, Sony's lawyers set to work, but as Mariah would find out, the wheels of justice would indeed grind slowly. Vian's case spent nearly a year in court before all charges against Mariah were dismissed. The case with Taber and Gonzalez dragged on for years before being decided in Mariah's favor.

But Mariah was too caught up in the success of *Emotions* and her growing love life with Tommy to spend too much time worrying about court cases. In many quarters, *Emotions*, as divergent a sounding record as *Mariah Carey* was one note, was suffering unfairly by comparison. "Can't Let Go," the second single from *Emotions* made it to only number two on the *Billboard* charts, which many considered a disappointment. *Emotions* had sold three million copies by the end of 1991 — a pretty respectable hit, but because that was only half of what *Mariah Carey* had sold in the same period a year earlier, skeptics amazingly marked the album a commercial failure! For her part, Mariah refused to play the numbers game, pointing instead to the album's accomplishments in the areas of soul, jazz, gospel, and R&B and the fact that she had avoided repeating the formula that had worked for her on *Mariah Carey*. The latter accomplishment was particularly important to Mariah. She was perceptive enough to know that any form of music was subject to becoming a formula, and that her small steps away from the gloss had been a major step forward for her as an artist.

Once again, the call went out for Mariah to tour. The requests were heard most consistently from her record company which felt that touring was the only way to jump-start what they already perceived as lagging sales for *Emotions*. Mariah was still not ready to take that step. She would explain to anyone who would listen that she was still very much an introvert who enjoyed creating her own little world in the studio.

It had been assumed that Mariah would be nominated for the 1992 Grammys, but given the sluggish sales of *Emotions* compared to her debut and the mediocre reception the album had received from critics, the odds were against anything approaching the multiple nods from the previous year. *Emotions* received one nomination for Best Producer for Mariah and Walter Afanasieff but ended up failing to capture the award in that category.

Shortly after the Grammys, the third and final single off *Emotions*,

"Make It Happen," was released and, like its predecessors, struggled to a number five slot. Again, that was nothing to sneeze at, but to the number crunchers in the Sony tower, it was a sign that something was wrong and needed to be fixed. Mariah didn't think so and was secure in her status as pop star. "If I wanted to stay home and write songs and make a moderate living, I could do that," she said in *New York* magazine in the wake of *Emotions'* mediocre showing. "I'm not worried that I might have to go back and waitress." Mariah had become completely confident in herself, and that's all that really mattered.

CHAPTER SIX

All Work
and All Play

Despite the critical attacks leveled at *Emotions*, the record was already well on its way to multiplatinum success and proving to be a slow but steady seller. As sophomore efforts went, *Emotions* was a solid progression that had successfully avoided the second-album jinx which had felled so many other artists.

Mariah had been working nonstop for nearly two years, and although it did not show on the surface, the consensus of those around her was that she was tiring. Nobody would have blamed Mariah if she had taken a long and well-deserved vacation. But that was not Mariah. A vacation for her was going to the studio at every opportunity and playing around with new lyrics and arrangements. Walter Afanasieff, when he was not busy on other projects, would inevitably drop by, and the pair would once again pick up on what had become a comfortable and productive relationship. Although he would never admit it, the speculation around the industry was that Walter, who had made the leap from talented unknown to bona fide hit-maker on the strength of his work with Mariah, felt a little proprietary when it came to her. Her voice was a tool for him to make studio magic. Even if that were the case, Mariah felt that Walter was a key element of her music and her enthusiasm, and believed he would always be an integral part of her music life.

Mariah, admittedly, did not really know what direction her next album should take. She had been quite happy with the back-to-basics approach of *Emotions* and felt part of that sound would remain. She also conceded

Singing on *MTV Unplugged* in 1992
FRANK FORCINO / LONDON FEATURES

that a certain amount of polish and orchestration was necessary, but, as always, she strove not to repeat herself. So, while some songs began to come together in the early days of 1992, nothing was definite.

Nothing was definite, that is, except for the growing relationship with Tommy Mottola. That was very much a love match, although Mariah would occasionally giggle and admit that lust had a lot to do with it as well and that Tommy was quite the lover. She was also quite adamant in explaining that her relationship with Tommy "represented a form of stability that I'd never had." The ink had barely dried on Mottola's divorce decree when the tabloids and gossip columns began speculating about when the Hollywood power couple would make it legal and tie the knot. Mottola had little to say on the subject, and Mariah would say only that she was not ready for marriage yet. A big reason was her relative youth and the fact that "I hadn't experienced much of life itself." But when pressed, she would acknowledge that "When my parents got divorced and I saw all my friends' parents getting divorced, it kind of hardened me to the idea of getting married." Given all the emotional baggage from her childhood and her relative inexperience in many facets of life, people were left to wonder why Mariah would get involved in a monogamous relationship when she was finally in a position to spread her wings. Many observers of Mariah's relationship with Tommy were concerned that it might ultimately turn from love to control and wondered how Mariah would respond to that. But one need only look at the happiness on Mariah's face when she was with Tommy to conclude that the relationship was truly working.

Mariah was very much a New York girl by this time. She was totally involved in the lifestyle, the business, and the rhythm of the streets. It was a given that her circle of friends would grow to include primarily local people. But Mariah was the first to admit that it was not by design. Sadly, but not unexpectedly, her friends from high school on Long Island had slowly begun to fall by the wayside, but it was not all Mariah's doing. During her first years in the city, she made a conscious effort to keep in touch. However, the time spent with old friends was often uncomfortable. Mariah had been branded a star, and friends from the old neighborhood could not help but perceive and treat her differently, alternating between fawning and patronizing. On the other hand, her city friends, perhaps a bit more sophisticated to the ways of showbiz, took her celebrity in stride and treated her as just plain Mariah. She sadly acknowledged that when it came to her circle of friends, she was now in a different world.

The calls for Mariah to tour continued, and when she once again refused, skeptics began to repeat the taunts that Mariah was a total studio creation who did not have the talent (despite her sporadic appearances on award shows) to carry off a full-blown live concert on her own. These charges were frustrating for Mariah — frustrating as well as uncomfortable. Her worst nightmare had always been about not being able to work her magic in a live setting. To have it constantly bandied about in the press only seemed to add to her discomfort and doubt. She now felt that it was imperative for her to do a live show — and soon. MTV's Unplugged series seemed to offer the perfect compromise. It would be a live concert, but it would be only thirty minutes long in front of a relatively small audience, and it would ultimately be seen by millions over repeated showings on the music video station. And far from the relative sterility of the studio, she would be working with real musicians rather than synthesizers and drum machines.

That Mariah would sing her hits during the Unplugged set was a given. But Mariah wanted to make her coming out something special, and so, just days before the March 16 taping at New York's Kaufman Astoria Studios,

Mariah and Walter went into the studio and put together a soulful rendition of "I'll Be There," the Berry Gordy-penned song by The Jackson Five that would feature Mariah in a duet with her good friend, singer Trey Lorenz. Although she admitted to being very nervous backstage before the taping began, Mariah quickly warmed to the relative intimacy of the Unplugged set and the enthusiastic audience. She was alternately upbeat, playful, and soulful as she ran through a miniset of her big hits. She was all smiles as she walked offstage at the conclusion of the taping, and she felt she had accomplished something in this live setting. Suddenly, the idea of touring on a grand scale did not seem quite so out of the question.

Mariah assumed that MTV would air the concert from time to time throughout the coming months and that would be the end of it. But the initial response to Mariah's Unplugged performance was so overwhelming that MTV immediately began showing the concert on a regular basis. Fans had gone particularly wild over Mariah's version of "I'll Be There," and so it was suggested by the bottom-line people at Sony that it might be a good idea to rush-release a single of her performance. The next logical step seemed to be to release an EP containing Mariah's seven-song live performance. Sony decided to do both. On May 28, "I'll Be There" debuted at number thirteen on the *Billboard* charts, the highest chart debut in Mariah's career. By June 20, the single made it to number one and would stay there for two weeks. *Mariah Carey: MTV Unplugged* was released in late June and made a rapid ascent to number three. Mariah, in the spirit of payback for this unexpected success, insisted that a portion of the sales from the EP, which would ultimately sell more than two million copies in a matter of months, be given to a number of charities. *MTV Unplugged* appeared on the surface to be nothing more than a stopgap measure to appease fans until the release of the next Mariah Carey studio album. But the reality was that the EP effectively captured Mariah in transition. The renditions of her signature songs live for the first time in even this subdued concert setting showed the singer growing in confidence as a performer. Mariah was comfortable with her songs and was subtly playful at a time when all that was asked of her was rote interpretations. And remaking "I'll Be There" was, commercially speaking, a stroke of genius. Having a ready-made, radio-friendly single automatically made *MTV Unplugged* more than a dolled-up greatest-hits package and something akin to an event.

Mariah, in the wake of her MTV smash, continued to be a benefactor.

As a result of the success of "I'll Be There," Trey Lorenz was offered a recording contract by Epic Records. Mariah, who should have been working on her next album, dropped everything to devote the next three months to helping Trey on his debut album. With the aid of Walter Afanasieff, she either produced or coproduced five tracks on the album and cowrote two of the songs: "Someone to Hold" and "Always in Love." It was an enjoyable and challenging process for Mariah, and her success as a first-time producer had whet her appetite to produce and write on other artists' records. In fact, her second outside gig would come sooner than expected. Daryl Hall, of the famed white soul duo Hall and Oates, was gearing up for a solo project entitled *Soul Alone* and was looking for outside material. Mariah took the leap, and acting purely as a songwriter, wrote "Help Me Find a Way to Your Heart," which ended up on the album. Mariah Carey's career was growing by leaps and bounds, and her personal life was also about to take a mighty step forward.

Mariah had not seen it coming, but in December 1992, Tommy Mottola asked Mariah Carey to be his wife. "It was very romantic," Mariah said of Tommy's proposal in a *TV Hits* magazine interview. "He's a very romantic person." Mariah did not have to think very long before she said yes. She knew she had a lot of resistance to the institution of marriage, but in the face of Tommy's truly loving and romantic nature, how could she say no? "I guess I finally realized that marriage doesn't have to be so bad," she recalled of her decision in *Ebony* magazine. Tommy and Mariah agreed that a traditional June marriage would allow them to finish up their professional duties and leave them time for a long honeymoon. They did not take any pains to hide their pending nuptials, and so it was not long before Tommy and Mariah found themselves all over the front page. There were the expected good wishes as well as the smattering of negativity directed toward Mariah. Some wags charged that her marriage to Mottola was nothing more than a career move to solidify her stature at Sony Records. Mariah, who normally let negativity roll off her back, bristled at the charge, which she vehemently denied in an interview with *TV Hits*. "All I can say is that I had a lot of success before we decided to get married. Somebody as powerful as Tommy can help people get started, but they can't make people sell millions of records."

As with her previous projects, Mariah's state of mind was integral to her approach to making her next album. Tommy had popped the question shortly before Mariah was scheduled to enter the studio. With Mariah so obviously in love, the feeling was that *Music Box* was going to be a light, pop-flavoured outing, heavy on glossy production and light on messages. But as production began in earnest, Mariah indicated that *Music Box* was going to be a much more subtle progression. The songs would range farther afield to incorporate even more disparate elements of soul, jazz, and gospel. Her upper-register vocals, an admitted trademark by this time, would be more subtle. She conceded that the album would contain some light, up-tempo songs, but that by her standards, it would contain more substantial, defining moments.

By the time *Music Box* was in production, Mariah actually admitted that she was looking forward to working with another set of gifted producer-songwriters. By this time, this had become a given on all of Mariah's albums. Returning from *Emotions* were Afanasieff, Clivillés, and Cole. Coming into Mariah's world for the first time were David Hall and Babyface; the latter, whose real name is Kenneth Edmonds, was just beginning to come into his own as a multifaceted upper-echelon producer, writer, and performer. One of the earliest songs to come out of these sessions was the spirited, up-beat pop ditty "Dreamlover," which in its final form, would project a kind of retro fifties feel that appealed to Mariah.

Encouraged by the success of *Emotions* and MTV *Unplugged*, Mariah decided that this album would be a hybrid — leaning toward the basic R&B feel while not forgetting the orchestration and polish of her debut album. Lyrically, the songs would carry the same reflective feel of her previous music. But the memory of her successful remake of "I'll Be There" had also made her aware of the commercial potential of redoing an oldie but goldie. This time, Mariah chose to go back once again to the seventies with the song "Without You," which was a big hit in the seventies for pop singer Harry Nilsson, and which was written by members of the sixties rock group Badfinger. Mariah had been enamored of the power behind the simple lyrics of the original and felt she could bring that gem successfully into the nineties. But, as always seemed to happen in a Mariah Carey recording session, there would be one big surprise along the way.

Epic Records had picked up the plumb deal to do the soundtrack for the upcoming Dustin Hoffman–Geena Davis movie *Hero*. At the head of their wish list for the album was a song called "Hero" sung by Mariah. But Mariah was working on *Music Box* at the time, and Sony was nervous about their top singer contributing something to an album by a competing label, even if that label was under the same corporate umbrella. The folks at Epic did not give up that easily and opted for an alternative plan in which Mariah would write the song even if she did not perform it. Walter Afanasieff screened the movie to get a feeling for the song. One day, during a break in working on *Music Box*, Mariah and Afanasieff sat down at the piano and within a space of a couple of hours, had come up with a thick, overly dramatic and, to their way of thinking, very un-Mariahlike ballad called "Hero." As luck would have it, Tommy had come down to the studio the day they were putting the finishing touches on "Hero," heard a very rough demo of the song, and promptly insisted that Mariah had to do it for her next album. Afanasieff reported back to Epic with the white lie that he had been unable to come up with a song. "Hero," with a radically reworked arrangement that emphasized Mariah's strengths, became one of the most powerful tracks on *Music Box*, which was completed in the spring and scheduled for a late summer release.

Now it was time to get married. Mariah wanted a traditional wedding, but when it came to traditional, she did not have a clue. "I didn't know anything about traditions because I wasn't one of those girls who grew up thinking about getting married," she told *US*. Finally, she decided that the wedding of Princess Di and Prince Charles was similar to the type of tradition and fantasy that she wanted for her own special moment, and she watched tapes of that lavish ceremony a number of times to get some ideas that she could incorporate into her big day. Although they were not royalty, Tommy and Mariah did not have to worry about paying for their traditional wedding. Money was no object, and Mariah, who had grown up around few of the niceties of life, was going to spend like there was no tomorrow. Her custom-made Vera Wang wedding dress, complete with a twenty-seven-foot train and ten-foot-long veil, reportedly came to somewhere in the vicinity of $25,000. Likewise, a pair of wedding shoes from famed shoe designer Vanessa Noel cost $1,000.

But it was the small things that meant the most to Mariah. The gown had taken care of the something new. Something old was an English sixpence, a family heirloom, which she put inside one of her shoes. Something borrowed was another old family heirloom, a tiara, which she had redesigned into a replica of the one Princess Diana wore. And something blue? Well rumor had it that it was a garter, but nobody knew for sure. That would

Mariah marries Tommy Mottola in June 1993

be the part of the wedding that would always remain a secret. The rest of the wedding was anything but. Word of the Mottola-Carey nuptials was once again the top entertainment story around the world. Mariah and Tommy had always known that they could not keep their plans a secret, but they took great pains to keep it as private as possible. Access to the church ceremony and the party afterward would be restricted — a two-hundred-member private security force would be enforcing their privacy. Given Tommy's influence in the entertainment industry, it did not come as a surprise to Mariah that the three hundred invited guests — a who's who of the music industry — included such diverse personalities as Ozzy Osbourne, Barbra Streisand, Billy Joel, Gloria Estefan, and Dick Clark.

Putting the finishing touches on *Music Box* had been a welcome distraction from the wedding plans, but with the completion of the album, Mariah grew increasingly tense as the big day approached. She was not sleeping well, and while no one believed that she was having second thoughts, were the wedding day jitters another form of her old stage fright? "I wasn't nervous about the wedding. But I was afraid that I would be walking down the aisle and trip," she once said. "The night before the wedding, I did not sleep at all. I spent the night hanging out with my brides-maids in our hotel suite."

On the morning of her wedding, Mariah looked out her hotel window at darkening skies and the promise of rain, not the best omen to begin a new life with the man she loved. But Mariah had long ago stopped being superstitious, and so, as she got into her bridal gown, the only thing she was visualizing was blue skies and sunny days. Mariah's limo drove slowly down the New York streets, rounded a corner, and pulled up in front of the St. Thomas Episcopal Church. The skies had indeed opened up but rather than a downpour, had produced only a drizzle. Mariah was happily surprised to see hundreds of fans along with the expected clusters of photographers cheering her arrival. She struggled out of the limo and with the aid of half a dozen ladies-in-waiting, maneuvered her way into the church. The marriage ceremony was brief. Their vows, heartfelt and sincere. The pronouncements were full of good cheer and bright hope for Tommy and Mariah's life together. At the words "You may kiss the bride," Tommy turned and kissed Mariah for the first time as his wife. They turned and walked hand in hand down the aisle, out of the church, once again through the multitude of cheering fans and flashing cameras, and into the waiting limo that would take the happy couple over to the exclusive Metropolitan Club where the bride and groom would party the night away.

The music at the party was a mixture of the couple's favorites. Tommy favored old-school Motown, while Mariah grooved to the driving beat of seventies disco. None of Mariah's own music was played at the wedding reception, and at no point did she even consider the idea of singing. This was her day to be young, in love, and happily married, and she was not going to let even the slightest bit of her professional life seep into the proceedings. In between greeting their guests, Mariah and Tommy would hit the dance floor, smiles permanently etched on their faces as they whirled around to such songs as The Dixie Cups' "Going to the Chapel" and Stevie Wonder's "You and I." After hours of dancing, eating, drinking champagne, and being with friends and family, Mariah and Tommy said their good-byes and were off to a limo that would whisk them to the airport and their extended honeymoon in Hawaii. As they were leaving, Mariah realized that she had not yet thrown the bridal bouquet. She wanted the time-honored tradition to be special. "There were these fans standing outside the club when we were leaving," recalled Mariah in an interview with *TV Hits*. "They had been standing out there all night, and so I decided to throw it to them. I didn't find out who caught it until much later when I saw this picture of this hysterical girl."

The time in Hawaii was a relaxing break from the couple's hectic working lives. They slept late, relaxed on the beach, and made love often. By the time the couple returned from Hawaii, Mariah was emotionally at peace. She was happy and content in her new life as wife. No longer did she have the insecurities surrounding the institution of marriage. She no longer felt, as many of her peers had, that marriage was somehow the end of the road. From where she was standing, marriage to Tommy was only the beginning, and the future looked bright. "When I look back and think about it, it's so unbelievable," Mariah gushed to *People* magazine. "I mean, it really is like Cinderella."

Upon their return to New York, the newlyweds quickly settled into two residences. Since so much of their time was centered in New York City, they wisely decided to take an apartment in the upper west side of Manhattan. But the home that Mariah favored was the comfortable and spacious estate in Bedford in upstate New York. That home, located in the Hudson River Valley, was very country in tone and appealed to Mariah's sense of getting away from it all. She would spend many happy hours in the many rooms — when she could find the time.

But, with the memories of her wedding day and honeymoon still fresh in her thoughts, it was time to go back to work. The promotion machine was once again in high gear in anticipation of the September 17 release of *Music Box*, which, for Mariah, meant making another video of the first single off the album, "Dreamlover." There was also the expected round of publicity interviews, which, not unexpectedly, prominently featured the topic of her recent marriage. Mariah launched into the promotion of the album with a sense of joy and purpose. *Music Box*, with its signs of lyrical and vocal maturity, was an album she was truly proud of, and she was going to do everything in her power to help make it a smash. Most observers of the music scene looked at the arrival of *Music Box* as a pivotal point in Mariah Carey's career. For all the plaudits for *MTV Unplugged*, the fact remained that it did not succeed in erasing the lukewarm reception accorded to *Emotions*. If *Music Box* was not a critical as well as commercial success, there was the danger that Mariah would be perceived ultimately as a slight artist with commercial potential but limited artistic prospects.

"Dreamlover" was released on August 13, 1993. The single debuted at number thirteen on the *Billboard* charts, and, fueled by a massive amount of radio airplay, the song raced to the number one slot in three weeks. Critically speaking, "Dreamlover" was a slight piece of pop fluff following more on the strictly commercial heels of "I'll Be There" than the more ambitious "Vision of Love." But it was still summer, and people were looking for a not-too-heavy diversion when they turned on the radio. And so, to the surprise of many who expected "Dreamlover" to have a short stay at number one, the song went on to hold the top spot for a total of eight weeks.

Music Box was an entirely different story. The album debuted on the album charts in late September and began a slow, steady climb — with the emphasis on *slow*. For whatever reason and especially following on the heels of her *MTV Unplugged*, the CDs were not flying out of the stores as they had in the past. To a large extent, the answer lay with the critics who absolutely savaged the album. Reviewers were lining up to say that *Music Box* did not contain much emotion and passion. There was a particular amount of abuse leveled at Mariah's decision to pull back on her vocals, saying that in many cases, without her soaring voice, the often sparse arrangements and instrumentation were fairly lifeless. Mariah was disappointed at the album's critical reception but not overly surprised. She had seen the signs of a backlash forming all the way back to the time of the release of *Emotions*. She recognized the fact that being an admitted pop singer had always made her an easy target, and that her relationship with Tommy had engendered a number of jealousies in the music community that would lead to blanket pans of her work. So she took the smattering of good reviews with her trademark graciousness and basically ignored the rest.

In retrospect, *Music Box* is arguably one of Mariah's most risky experiments. Rather than soar on the strength of her trademark multi-octave singing, on nearly all the cuts she brought things down to a surprisingly subdued level. It was as if she decided to let the songs sink or swim on their lyrical merit alone. And the result was a decidedly mixed bag. "Dreamlover" was the hands-down continuation of Mariah's commercial savvy — mid-tempo, mildly danceable, with a slight R&B feel, and the singer's perpetually happy, little-girl voice. A whole album of this kind of material no doubt would have had its detractors, but "Dreamlover," followed by the maudlin but radio-friendly "Hero" made a strong case for her pop instincts.

Following up the remake success of "I'll Be There" with "Without You" not only hedged her bet for another hit single, but it also gave Mariah the chance to do more theatrical and dramatic stylings that would most certainly come into play in the coming years. The remaining tracks, a mixture of pop ballads and light dance numbers, put the emphasis on tiny arrangements with a decidedly R&B feel. Lyrically, R&B was not always Mariah's strength, for while the songs were nothing if not direct, many of them seemed to be making small efforts to tell simple stories. In the end, that left the critics feeling that some of the songs on *Music Box* were slight and lacked ambition. Music historians will most likely relegate *Music Box* to a bottom rung of Mariah Carey's creative ladder. But the better moments of the album indicate that she was making an attempt, albeit small, to push the envelope. But record buyers were, for the most part, ignoring the critics, and *Music Box* quickly became platinum. If not a critical victory, Mariah at least saw the success of *Music Box* as a commercially viable one. "As soon as you have a big success, a lot of people don't like that," she said in a candid *Vogue* interview. "There's nothing I can do about it. All I can do is make music that I believe in."

Mariah's life continued in a constant swirl. There were endless hours on the promotion trail. When she had the time, Mariah would inevitably steal away into a recording studio and just play around with lyrics and arrangements, already thinking in terms of the next step. But despite their busy lives, Tommy and Mariah would regularly try to get away to their upstate retreat where they continued to act like they were on their honeymoon. "We're just right for each other," said Mariah, "and that's all that matters." However, Mariah admitted that there were the occasional arguments over creative decisions. This highlighted the fact that despite her denials, there was some rough moments that were very much age-related. "We do sometimes get into fights over business," she told *People*. "He's ready to say 'do it this way,' and I'm very independent."

Tommy and Mariah continued to be hot copy in the weeks and months following their marriage. With Mariah at the top of her career and with her personal life together, the rumors soon began to fly that she was going to take some time off, and that she and Tommy were trying to have a baby. However, Mariah laughed off that notion in *US* magazine. "A baby? Not for a long time. I wouldn't want to be one of those people who gives my child to a nanny to raise." Mariah Carey may not have been ready for motherhood just yet, but she definitely was ready for something else. Fingering her lucky ring, she decided that she was ready to tour.

CHAPTER SEVEN

Star-Spangled Road Stories

Going on tour for the first time was not a spur-of-the-moment decision. By the time she was putting the finishing touches on *Music Box*, plans for Mariah to go live were already in the works. She would never actually reveal what the reasons were for suddenly overcoming her stage fright, but one theory was that after nearly four years of nonstop studio work, she was getting cabin fever. Another was that Mariah was curious about how her music would sound in a huge concert venue in front of thousands of fans. But the consensus of those around Mariah was that her surprising ease in front of an audience during the taping of her *Unplugged* show as well as the increasing lack of nerves in her handful of television and award-show appearances over the past two years had finally given her the confidence to test the waters in performance.

Tommy was thrilled at Mariah's change of heart. From a creative as well as financial point of view, touring was important to the longevity of her career and her continued popularity. But Mariah made it clear that she was not ready for the physical and emotional demands of an extensive tour that would last for months. To her way of thinking, a dozen dates would be stretching her endurance — six shows, she reasoned, would be much more manageable. And so, Sony set about dealing with a number of promoters who were falling over themselves to be a part of Mariah's first tour. It would not be an extensive one, totaling just five dates in Miami, Florida, Worcester, Massachusetts, Rosemont, Illinois, Philadelphia, and New York City. The shows would not be on consecutive nights in order to give Mariah the chance to rest up and retool between performances. She immediately began an extensive round of rehearsals after recruiting a stellar cast of musicians. She worked out the kinks — known as "wood-shedding" in the biz — in the studio, crafting a strong live set that she would feel comfortable taking on the road and that would have the biggest impact. It was a given that Mariah's first concert tour would be made up primarily of her best-known songs, the radio-friendly hits that had paved her way to the top. But she was also eagerly looking forward to the prospect of slipping in a hand-ful of songs that had not made the commercial cut but that she considered worthy of public exposure.

Meanwhile behind the scenes, Mariah's management team was looking for new ways to promote their superstar, and in late summer they negoti-ated a deal with NBC television for a one-hour Mariah Carey special to be aired in November. Mariah warmed to the idea of the traditional variety show, which would have lots of singing, some dancing, and numerous costume changes. It would allow Mariah and her band to rehearse her up-coming concert set in a fairly relaxed atmosphere. It would also give Sony a chance to tape the concert for a video that would be rushed onto the market in time for Christmas. The Mariah Carey television special was filmed in the Proctor Theater in upstate New York, not far from Mariah and Tommy's new estate. That made for an easy commute and a more relaxed Mariah. The night of the taping, the theater was packed to the rafters with enthusiastic fans, many of whom carried signs with messages for the singer. Backstage, Mariah was calm and upbeat and with good reason — she had an escape hatch. Since the show was being filmed for later airing, they could cover up any flaws in the performance with a retake and judicious editing. She was also feeling comfortable because the show's director, Larry Jordan, had worked with her on a number of videos as well as the *MTV Unplugged* show. Although it would be a one-hour special, the stop-and-start nature of filming would mean many hours of work to complete the project. This would, to her way of thinking, be the closest she would ever come to a perfect performance, and Mariah was pleased with that notion.

The Mariah Carey television special turned out to be a spirited musical exercise on Mariah's part. Rather than just trot out her greatest-hits package for the camera, she chose to mix things up with moments of humor and a flamboyant approach to the show. The singer, who has admitted that she was not much of a dancer, nevertheless found that her band had set up an easy groove to which she could smoothly move around the stage. There were the inevitable breaks between songs as Mariah would disappear for a costume change while stagehands rearranged microphones and set up new backdrops. But, despite the mechanical, jerky stop-and-go nature of the filming, Mariah came off as a polished performer who could take command of the stage and move the audience with her songs. She emerged from the filming of the television special confident that she could move from entertaining the T.V. audience of a few hundred to the upcoming concert tour at which she would be performing in front of thousands.

However, word of Mariah's tour did not result in a mad rush for tickets, and there was some apprehension when it didn't sell out overnight. But sales were steady and almost all the shows sold out within a couple of weeks. Mariah's energy level was high as she made the final preparations for the tour. She was confident that she was up to the task, but only time would tell if she was right. The first stop on Mariah's exploratory minitour was Miami Arena. It was about two-thirds full on November 3, 1993. The record execs were worried by the fact that her first show was not completely sold out, but Mariah put a positive spin on things, saying that she preferred it this way because it made the show feel more intimate. She was encouraged by the fact that rather than a largely teen audience, which was her perceived fan base, the Miami show attracted many young couples. As Mariah prepared to take the stage, the first-night jitters she had experienced in the past returned. "I was okay until I had to walk up this big ramp to the stage," she recalled in a Q magazine interview. "Then I heard this deafening scream, and it was like everything in my life had all been leading up to this insane moment and there I was."

The show lasted seventy-five minutes and it was a bit of a rollercoaster ride, with both high and low points for the singer. On the plus side, Mariah was comfortable when she was singing, and the audience was treated to a spirited mixture of her hits as well as a variety of album cuts and the odd cover tunes. They saw a confident Mariah whose voice and songs struck an emotional chord with the appreciative fans in attendance. And, as she showed in the NBC T.V. special, Mariah was in command of the stage, moving from side to side and acknowledging the fans while doing a variety of subtle moves. But then the roller coaster dipped and there was the downside of the performance. When she was not singing, Mariah looked like the proverbial deer caught in the headlights. Her nervousness was betrayed by the forced between-song patter that she kept to a bare minimum and seemed anything but natural. However, by the time Mariah stepped out for the final encore of the evening, she felt that the audience was in her corner. She believed they knew that this was her first big live show and were supportive. "I think I sang well in Miami," she would relate to the *Los Angeles Times* after the tour was over. "I did the best show that I could."

But, as she climbed into her limo and drove back to her hotel following the concert, Mariah knew — she just knew — that the critics would not be as kind as her fans. Her premonition was correct — Miami was a critical disaster. Mariah would later recall that the reviewers, both local and national, had ripped her opening-night performance to shreds. And Mariah had to admit that by her own high standards the Florida show was shaky. But the true impact of her first live concert hit her the hardest that night in her hotel room when she was lying on her bed watching CNN. The entertainment reporter came on and said "Well, it's bad news for Mariah Carey." And he rattled off a litany of negative comments about her performance. For Mariah, it was the worst kind of slap in the face and her worst nightmare come true.

Mariah's confidence was shattered. She was upset, angry, and the worst part of all was that she would have a whole week to brood over the slights before her next scheduled concert. During those days, Mariah overcame everything but her anger. In a highly defensive posture, she lashed out, saying that she knew the critics had been waiting for an opportunity to get her, and that their attacks were part of a backlash against her. But once she calmed down, she decided that the best defense would be a good offense. She told *Q* magazine, "I decided I would put all my anger into it, let go of all my inhibitions, and just lose myself in the performance."

The November 9 show in The Centrum in Worcester, Massachusetts was sold out. And despite being the second stop on her tour, the packed house was rewarded with Mariah's unofficial coming-out party. That night, Mariah sang like she was hungry for the spotlight and the attention. Her voice echoed through the arena with a power and a passion that immediately pushed her performance to new heights. The insecurities that had marred the Miami show had disappeared, and in their stead, stood the

Daydream European Tour 1996

image of Mariah Carey as a masterful, confident live performer. Eight days later, she would prove that the Worcester show was no fluke when she wowed another sold out audience at Rosemont Horizon in Illinois with a show that continued to highlight Mariah's growing confidence and performing persona. Happily, she could no longer be dismissed as the "studio creation" who had "lucked into" or "married into" a career. In the eyes of the public and critics, Mariah Carey was a legitimate all-around performer who could walk the walk — and sing a mean song.

Mariah took a two-week break in mid-November to be with family and friends for Thanksgiving and to watch her long-anticipated television special. It aired on November 25 to rave reviews and monster ratings. The tour resumed in early December, with the final two shows at The Spectrum in Philadelphia and Madison Square Garden in New York. In those shows, Mariah showed a definite edge in her singing, and there were signs that she was developing a definite sexy "uptown" performing style to match the strength and range of her voice and the lyrical power of her songs. And when she finished up her New York show with an impromptu version of "Santa Claus Is Coming to Town," the signs all pointed toward the fact that in a space of five concerts, Mariah Carey had arrived. She was a superstar on the stage as well as in the studio. Consequently, Mariah Carey was in a festive mood as she celebrated with family and friends. Her first Christmas with Tommy as husband and wife continued the fairy-tale nature of their relationship with gifts, good cheer, and some quiet times. In fact, Mariah was so caught up in the Christmas spirit that unbeknownst to any but a close circle of friends, she ended the year in the recording studio with Walter Afanasieff recording a soulful version of "Silent Night." It was the first song for a Christmas album of traditional carols and brand-new tunes that Mariah hoped to have out in time for Christmas 1994.

The early months of the new year were a time of mixed emotions for Mariah. Things could not be better in her personal life — her bond with Tommy could not be stronger. But the Grammys once again proved to be a disappointment. "Dreamlover" was nominated for Best Song but did not win, and the album *Music Box*, despite being on track to ultimately sell more than twenty million copies, did not receive a single nomination. But Mariah salved her frustration when her second single, "Without You," was released late in January and went all the way to number three on the charts by March. A third and final single off the *Music Box* album, "Anytime You Need a Friend," was released in May and peaked at number twelve in June.

All the while, Mariah would continue to slip secretly into the studio, putting herself in a Christmas mood despite the fact that the calendar said spring and then summer. She and Walter wrote and recorded the original Christmas tunes "All I Want for Christmas Is You," "Jesus Born on This Day," and "Miss You Most (At Christmas Time)" as well as mellow versions of the time-honored classics "O Holy Night" and "Joy to the World."

When not working on that album, Mariah and Walter were already beginning to play around with material for her next studio album. It was during this period that Mariah became involved in what would be the latest round of a sporadic list of guest shots on other artist's records. At the time, Walter was producing an album for singer Luther Vandross and had chosen a remake of the song "Endless Love," which was originally a smash hit by Diana Ross and Lionel Richie. Mariah jumped at the chance to do a duet with Vandross, a singer she greatly admired. The song was released in early fall and climbed to number three on *Billboard*'s Hot 100 chart by late October. Shortly before its release on November 1, 1994, *Billboard* magazine lifted the veil on the secret of Mariah's Christmas present, the album entitled simply *Merry Christmas*. It was an interesting, if ultimately slight, effort. As Christmas albums go, Mariah's mixture of classics and originals was head-and-shoulders above most of those released by established artists that year. All of the songs benefited from Mariah's soulful vocals and from crisp arrangements. Make no mistake, this is a feel-good album that will be a perennial on radio stations for many Christmases to come. But it is far from important art. It was, however, like manna from heaven for the millions of Mariah Carey fans starved for anything new from their favorite diva — her latest album, *Music Box*, had been released in September 1993 — and so the album quickly climbed to number three. It was a joyous end to a wonderful year for Mariah Carey.

But storm clouds were beginning to gather. Allison Carey had not led the fairy-tale life. Pregnant, married, and divorced before the age of twenty, Mariah's older sister had turned to drugs and prostitution. Mariah and Allison had never been close, particularly after she left with her father following the parents' divorce. The sisters pretty much severed their relationship after Allison got married. The question of her older sister rarely came up in interviews, and when it did, Mariah would dance around the subject. They had little contact except occasionally through their mother. In the end, Mariah totally disapproved of her sister's lifestyle and had chosen not to be involved with her. But all that changed midway through 1995 when Mariah received a phone call from her mother with the sad news — Allison Carey had AIDS.

CHAPTER EIGHT

Trouble
in Paradise

"When I found out she had AIDS, I must have cried for days," Mariah confessed to *Bravo* magazine not too long after she discovered her sister had
contracted the incurable and ultimately fatal disease. When she stopped
crying, Mariah had to deal with a conflicting array of emotions over her
sister and her plight. A big part of her was just plain sad. She was also
forgiving of Allison's choices and the mistakes that had led her to prostitution and drugs and which had finally brought her to this point. Mariah was
not finding it difficult to comprehend that her sister was experiencing such
a difficult time. But there was also a lot of anger directed toward her sister,
and Mariah was not sure where that was coming from.

Making matters worse was the fact that Allison was so wrapped up in
her disease, continued drug dependency, and her downward spiraling
lifestyle that she was totally incapable of taking care of her son. And so
Mariah temporarily called her career to a halt to help her family. After much
hand-wringing and soul-searching, she and her mother tried to get her sister
some help. They offered to pay for Allison to get into a drug-treatment
program and to get her AIDS counseling so that she could learn to live with
the disease and possibly get some treatment. However, in the midst of her
self-pity and misdirected anger toward her family — in particular Mariah —
she wanted no part of their help. When she refused to get treatment for her
myriad problems, Mariah and Patricia took the next, admittedly drastic,
step and arranged for her son to come and live with Patricia. However, this
intervention came at a heavy price. The long-simmering anger and jealousy

that Allison directed at Mariah for what she felt was the favoritism shown her younger sister because of her talent finally boiled over. Despite Mariah's public insistence that they were patching things up, the relationship between the two sisters was, for all intents and purposes, over. "I haven't spoken to my sister in a long time, but I hope she's well," Mariah told *Time* magazine. "But everything seems to have worked itself out."

Mariah's problems did not end with her sister. Although she would continue to put up a positive front when it came to her marriage, later she would candidly admit that by 1995, there were already signs that she and Tommy were on shaky ground and that the image of Cinderella living happily ever after had faded. Mariah should have seen it coming. From the beginning, Tommy Mottola (as the head honcho at Sony) had had this thing about controlling every aspect of Mariah Carey's career. He brought in producers and writers to work on Mariah's sound. He even suggested what songs were best for her and who she should work with in the studio. Mariah has admitted to being controlled by Tommy, but early on, she was willing to go along with it for the sake of her career. "I used to be insecure and cautious, and so I would listen to what other people said," she told *Star* magazine. And so when Tommy nixed the idea of her wearing revealing clothing onstage, Mariah tended to agree. Consequently, despite having a killer body and the ego to want to show it off, during the early years, Mariah rarely appeared in a miniskirt or a low-cut top.

Despite the occasional experiments in her music, Mariah was constantly being reminded by Tommy or one of his handpicked handlers of what worked and why they should not attempt anything different. Tommy's control over his "discovery" was so complete that he even got to approve all interviews and would automatically eliminate any media that had ever presented Mariah in anything but the most positive light. Even those who made the media cut were often subjected to long, pre-interview grillings from the PR people, during which time reporters were given a list of "sensitive" questions that could not be asked. It got to the point where at least one Sony representative had to be with Mariah at all times. In looking back, she could remember the constant distraction of someone looking over her shoulder from the moment she signed with Sony. There was the day in 1994 when Mariah, being interviewed by a *Vogue* magazine writer, decided to make things interesting by driving around New York in her limo during their discussion. The limo was about to take off when two Sony employees appeared on the sidewalk and began frantically banging on the limo windows, wanting to know what she was doing and where she was going. Just as the vehicle pulled out into the street, one of the Sony people jumped into the front seat beside the limo driver. Mariah and the journalist felt that the Sony presence cramped their style, and so Mariah pressed what she called "her privacy button," which cut off all sound to the front seat.

The media began to pick up on these things. Descriptions of Tommy as Mariah's Svengali soon escalated to terms like control freak, and the idea that Mariah was the puppet being manipulated by Tommy was now being proclaimed throughout the media. People at Sony knew the reality of the relationship, but they liked their jobs too much to say anything negative about the boss. There were those occasional watercooler observations about how other acts on the label were not getting nearly the same amount of attention that Mariah got. Mariah's naiveté led her to believe that Tommy had only her best interests at heart, and so she let a lot of his controlling nature slide for the good of her career. But once they got married, she found that his possessiveness was beginning to intrude on their personal relationship as well. Prior to their marriage, Mariah would always boast that despite their age difference, Tommy was quite a hip dude and all-around cool guy. But they had hardly finished saying their "I dos" when she began to discover another side.

Mariah, in her early twenties, was now attempting to have the fun she did not have while growing up. More and more, she wanted to go into the big city and party at nightclubs with her peers — a loose amalgamation of hip musicians and producers, friends she had made in New York, and the occasional mate from her youth. On the other hand, Tommy began to show his age and preferred to stay at home in their mansion and have quiet dinners with his business acquaintances. And so, more often than not, Mariah acquiesced and would end up spending her nights at home, dying of boredom amid a wash of shoptalk and a lifestyle that was slowly smothering her. Mariah would later state that while the house "wasn't a prison," she would rarely leave it for the first couple of years of marriage. The tension between Tommy and Mariah began to grow. As chronicled in a *Vanity Fair* article, the couple began to argue at the drop of the hat. Curses — as well as the occasional object — flew back and forth. These arguments would often end up with Mariah locking herself in her room and cranking up a rap album on the stereo. Over the din, Tommy could be heard outside the door, pounding and shouting at her to stop. Amusing as those scenes may have seemed, in retrospect, Mariah could sense that the marriage was in trouble. "People just grow up and apart and continue to change," she told a New York Post reporter in December 1997. "And I guess we both changed. I know it wasn't just me."

The tensions began to escalate when Mariah announced that she wanted to take her music in yet another new direction when recording her latest album Daydream. On the surface, Daydream appeared to be more of the same stuff that had made her a superstar — a mixture of soulful ballads and pop-flavored dance numbers. But, perhaps inspired by the success of her first concerts and the nuances she gleaned from hearing herself in a live setting, the songs that she was fashioning with longtime collaborators Walter Afanasieff and David Hall had a more downbeat feel, and were more reflective, moody, and weary in tone. She seemed to be incorporating bits and pieces of hip-hop and rap that had, for the most part, been missing from her earlier albums. "I went into this phase of recording, recording, recording and doing it really fast," she told Time. "This time, I had more time, and I focused more on what I wanted to do."

One of the early choices for Daydream, the slightly up-tempo pop ballad "Fantasy," incorporated part of Tom Tom Club's "Genius of Love" because she felt it fit in with what she was doing. Tommy readily approved the song but had to bite his tongue when Mariah excitedly announced that the remix of the proposed first single off the album would also be produced by rapper mogul Sean "Puffy" Combs, and that Ol' Dirty Bastard of the gangsta rap group Wu-Tang Clan did a rap over part of the song. Mottola knew the bottom-line value of rap. It was a commodity that sold, but it was not his favorite kind of music, and he shuddered at the prospect of even a small element of that raw street music making any inroads into the safe and profitable music of Mariah. "Everybody was like 'What, are you crazy?'" Mariah said in Entertainment Weekly. "They're very nervous about breaking the formula. It works to have me sing a ballad onstage in a long dress with my hair up." An unidentified Sony staffer came to Tommy Mottola's defense in Entertainment Weekly, "Tommy's looking at it from a business stand-point. Tommy's not saying, don't make black music. He's saying, don't go totally left of what you've already built."

Reports like that succeeded only in muddying the waters. Mariah began to question whether Tommy was truly looking out for her career or Sony's bottom line. Instinctively, she began to pull back on the candor she had had with Tommy on her music. She would not hide anything she was doing, but she would not volunteer details unless he asked. Unfortunately, the normally fun times that they had spent discussing her music suddenly became tense and brusque. Tommy was only slightly less annoyed when during the writing sessions that produced the song "One Sweet Day," Mariah decided she wanted to do the song with the hot young group Boyz II Men. The group was excited by the music they were hearing and, coincidentally, had some lyrics they had been working on that fit Mariah's arrangements like a glove. Again, for Tommy, it was a control thing. After all, Mariah was a star, and she should not have to *share* a song with anybody else. But still attempting to put the best face on the situation, Mariah insisted that "as far as the music goes," she and Tommy were still very much in sync.

Easily the most adventurous step on an already progressive project by Mariah's standards was including a cover of the rock group Journey's "Open Arms" on *Daydream*. Toned-down arrangements and a glossy overall feel made this an interesting gamble whether or not it worked. Mariah was much more involved in *Daydream* than she had been in previous albums and was spending more and more time in the studio. Whether this was by design or, as people in her inner circle were speculating, to get away from Tommy was anybody's guess. But one thing was certain. Tommy Mottola's paranoia was growing by leaps and bounds.

As reported in *Stern* magazine, Tommy hired two bodyguards to follow Mariah everywhere, including right up to the bathroom door. Tommy began to listen in on all of Mariah's telephone conversations from a phone in another part of the house, and he would routinely go through her mail before he gave it to her. When Mariah expressed an interest in taking acting lessons, Mottola wouldn't hear about it, wanting nothing to interfere with her music. He left strict orders that the acting teacher should not be allowed in the house. He became so jealous of the attention — real or imagined — other men paid to his wife that he would automatically fire any good-looking, non-gay male dancers from her videos. *Vanity Fair* further cited unknown sources who stated that Mariah could leave the house only after getting Tommy's approval and that wherever she went, a car with the bodyguards would be right behind her. The *Star* tabloid reported that Tommy eventually became so concerned about Mariah hanging around

Mariah with LL Cool J
KEVIN MAZUR / LONDON FEATURES

with rappers, even in the recording studio, that he had visions of her in the middle of a rapper shoot-out. He increased the number of bodyguards to five. Mariah suddenly came to the realization that not only had the love and friendship gone out of their marriage, but the trust as well.

The sadness and the confusing emotions she was feeling toward Tommy and their marriage were channeled into the studio and *Daydream*. There was a decided melancholy, world-weary feel to many of the songs, and while this was a perfect fit for the direction Mariah was going in, to observers, the pain and the disappointment that were in Mariah's lyrics seemed to be coming from an all-too-real place. Mariah immersed herself in the rush of promotion for *Daydream*, which was scheduled for release in late October 1995. As a prelude, the single "Fantasy" was released on September 30 and immediately put Mariah back on the map. It *debuted* at number one on the *Billboard* charts and stayed there for two solid months. With "Fantasy" paving the way, *Daydream* also hit the number one spot on the day of its release.

Critics who seemed to be making a career of trashing her music were now singing the praises of *Daydream*, citing her growing prowess as a singer–songwriter and applauding the chances she was taking by moving in a new direction. As she had tried to do on some of her previous albums, Mariah was now taking definite steps away from the general image of her as a studio-created bland pop diva. The decidedly hip-hop feel of "Fantasy" was duplicated, to varying degrees, on a number of songs on the album. There was a feeling that Mariah's songwriting had matured, which was much in evidence in the soulfully sexy lyrics of many of the songs. "One Sweet Day," with its gospel shadings, was that happy exception to an album with cuts that reflected a previously unheard-of (from Mariah) resignation to the downbeat side of life. The one truly risky venture that does not quite come off was the remake of Journey's "Open Arms." The song ended up being grossly overarranged, the heavy orchestration forced Mariah to sing at a strident level. But not all experiments are successful, and, in this case, Mariah deserved credit for taking the chance. It goes without saying that Mariah's disintegrating marriage and internal struggles and fears at the prospect of possibly becoming single again had a major impact on her attitude going into *Daydream*. Whatever the inherent turmoil, *Daydream* succeeded in permanently removing the tag of caricature from around Mariah Carey's neck.

During this period, Mariah performed on the Babyface song "Every Time I Close My Eyes." Being around that producer–writer–performer — he has been called the all-everything — was the best kind of on-the-job training for Mariah. When she was not singing, she would literally hang over Babyface's shoulder, watching how he did what he did and filing the information away in her head for future reference.

Just prior to the release of *Daydream*, Mariah flew to England where she sang "Fantasy" on the influential music show *Top of the Pops* and duplicated the performance for Asian television. The response to Mariah in Europe and Asia had always been good, and now, with the fantastic reviews coming from the continent, there was serious talk about Mariah doing her first world tour in 1996. The phenomenal success of *Daydream* continued when the follow-up single, "One Sweet Day," was released in early December. Like "Fantasy," it debuted at number one and stayed in the top spot for sixteen weeks.

The music industry took note of Mariah's success, and she and *Daydream* were nominated in six different categories for the annual 1995 Grammy Awards. And as befitting a multiple nominee, Mariah was invited to perform "One Sweet Day" live with Boyz II Men. Mariah had become a bit skittish about the idea of awards, feeling the pressure of having to justify her superstar status by winning every award in sight. And so, she was cautious when she discussed her prospects for the Grammys with *Billboard*.

"I didn't go into it with very high expectations," she said. "You can't pre-dict those things, and you can't control it. All you can do is be grateful for the nominations, go to the party, and have fun."

Mariah was in excellent spirits the night of the Grammys and was delighted at the applause she received for her soulful rendition of "One Sweet Day." But, as the night wore on and awards were handed out but Mariah wasn't called to the stage, the television cameras that were focused on her revealed the fact that it was getting harder for her to retain her smile. By the end of the night, with Mariah completely shut out, the disap-pointment on her face was obvious. Mariah and Tommy were off to a post-Grammy party, but the constant tension between the couple had only been exacerbated by her failure to win even one Grammy for what many critics openly proclaimed as the best album of the year. As reported in *Vanity Fair*, an argument broke out in the lobby of the hotel in which the party was being held. Mariah's anger and disappointment poured out of her as she turned on Tommy and accused him of not having enough power in the industry to get her a Grammy. Eventually, she quieted down, and the couple went into the party. But when Tommy discovered that video monitors at the party were playing back highlights of the awards, he ordered them switched off. Mariah eventually calmed down and was able to deal with her disappointment at her Grammy shutout. "What can you do?" she said later. "I will never be disappointed again. After sitting through the whole show and not winning once, I can handle anything."

Her growing interest in producing and developing new artists led Mariah to use her clout with Sony to start a subsidiary label to sign and develop new artists. Mariah's reasoning was that she had practical experi-ence in struggling and not having her efforts taken seriously and that she wanted to offer the opportunity for legitimate talent to be heard. Early in 1996, Sony agreed, and Crave Records became a reality. Of course, the cynics said that Crave was Tommy's way of getting back into Mariah's good graces after the Grammy debacle, and that the expected losses that Crave would generate could be written off as the cost of keeping the label's big-gest-selling artist happy. The first act signed to the subsidiary label was a hip-hop group called Blue Denim. Mariah was enthusiastic about this new opportunity, and while she personally attended to much of the corporate, administrative elements, she was at her best when she was dealing with the artists and producers as only another singer could. Studio sessions

Mariah Performs on *Top of the Pops*

MARK ALLEN / GLOBE PHOTOS

with her Crave artists would often turn into gab fests. Groups would sit fascinated as Mariah offered advice and a whole lot of stories that only somebody who had come through the music wars and survived could tell.

The promise of a world tour became a partial reality in March 1996 when Mariah flew to Japan to headline four sold-out concerts at The Tokyo Dome. The concerts were a critical success, and the reception Mariah received during her stay was so enthusiastic that parallels were drawn to the Beatlemania of the sixties. Mariah was on cloud nine. Then she returned to the states — and the reality of her disintegrating marriage to Tommy set in. Tommy's controlling nature had reached critical mass. When Mariah rekindled a just-friends relationship with an old high-school boyfriend, Tommy hit the ceiling. In response to the constant monitoring of her telephone conversations, Mariah and her friends had to begin speaking in code. Mariah was feeling so dominated that she resorted to small gestures of defiance such as styling her bangs in a way Tommy hated — anything to exert her dwindling independence. At one point, according to *Vanity Fair*, Mariah poured her heart out to Diana Ross about her problems when the pair shared a plane ride. Things had become so bad that Mariah's friends derisively began calling Mariah's upstate home "Sing Sing," a double pun referring to the prison-like nature of their relationship and the fact that

Tommy was always urging Mariah to sing. Tommy's controlling nature was evident in public situations as well. When the couple attended the 1996 Rock and Roll Hall of Fame induction ceremonies, the much-anticipated all-star jam had begun and Mariah was being urged by the other performers to join in. She started to get up out of her seat, but Tommy glared at her, shaking his head no. Mariah didn't want to cause a scene, so she was forced to sit down.

Mariah spent the spring months immersed in a number of projects. She began working in the studio with Blue Denim and started active rehearsals for the long-anticipated European summer tour that would take her into England, France, Holland, and Germany. The European tour mirrored the success of her shows in Japan. Mariah's appearances overseas were heartening experiences for the singer. The popularity — indeed, mania — surrounding her shows in these countries reached massive proportions. The reception the concerts received reflected the fact that Mariah's music cut through race and language barriers and had struck at a universal, emotional core with fans. The tours cemented the fact that Mariah Carey had arrived as the performing centerpiece on the world stage. It was also a time of freedom for the singer. She was now quite comfortable performing onstage and was using the applause and rave reviews as an emotional release from her problems back home. During the European tour, Mariah had time to think about her life and career. She had grown as a performer and was one of the reigning superstars of the nineties. And she was beginning to grow as a person, but now she had to decide on her next step. She completed the European tour in June and returned to the United States. She spent the winter months in quiet contemplation and with the exception of some preliminary studio work on songs for her next album, pondered the future.

A big part of her still respected Tommy and would be eternally grateful to him for what he had done for her career. And yes, a big part of her still loved him, but love, in this case, was not turning out to be enough. Shortly before Christmas 1996, Mariah moved out of the mansion of her dreams. She would never be back.

Chatting with Luciano Pavarotti

Performing with Boyz II Men's Wayna Morris at the 1996 Grammys

Hanging out with model Tyson Beckford

CHAPTER NINE

The Big Break

The transition from married to single life was a slow and deliberate one for Mariah. It started with a move to the city and temporary residence in a hotel. When she announced to Tommy that she was leaving, the expected blowup did not come. He made the expected overtures about her staying and their trying to work things out, but whether he felt that the separation would only be temporary or he had, in fact, likewise given up on the marriage, he did not try to stop her.

Those first nights alone in the big city were not easy for Mariah. For better or for worse, her years with Tommy had, if nothing else, given her a warm body, intelligent conversation, and, for the most part, a winning personality that helped shape her view of the world and of herself. Now that she was alone, all the little insecurities began rushing back. But they did not linger very long because Mariah felt that she was now fully capable of moving on and standing on her own two feet. Mariah began to take stock of her life, and she soon noticed how it was changing. Friends she had not seen much of when she was married to Tommy suddenly started coming around again. These were not the music moguls and corporate suits that she had mixed with during those years she was married to Tommy. These were musicians, actors, and just plain people from the 'hood — people she felt comfortable around, people she wholeheartedly welcomed back into her life. The vibe around Mariah had suddenly turned mellow, and she was quite happy with the change.

As expected, the tabloids had a field day with Mariah and Tommy's

separation, and all sorts of stories — some true and some flat-out fabrica-
tions — were plastered all over the papers. First out of the box were reports that the marriage was definitely over. These were followed by blaring
headlines that it was only a trial separation and that they would eventually
get back together. Then there were the ridiculous tales stating that Mariah
and Tommy were seen in romantic clinches in different New York hot spots.
There were also stories that Tommy and Mariah were already seeing other
people. Mariah's sense of confusion immediately after the separation only
succeeded in fueling the speculation. "You never know what may happen
in the future (between us)," she waffled in a *What's On* magazine in 1997.
"I don't believe in closing doors. I'm still hopeful we'll be able to work it
out."

But in the meantime, Mariah had quite a bit on her plate to keep her
busy. She was continuing to spend time in the studio with her Crave label
acts and was quite optimistic about the prospects for the fledgling group
Allure, to whom she contributed the songs "Head Over Heels" and "Last
Chance." For the group Blaque, she wrote the lyrics and produced the song
"After." Mariah was saddened to hear about the untimely death of Princess
Diana but was thrilled when asked to contribute a live version of "Hero"
to the *Princess Diana Tribute Album*. With friend Trey Lorenz, she sang the
song "Can Make You Happy," which would appear on the *Men in Black*
soundtrack album. She was also recruiting an eclectic cast of producers, musicians, and writers for her upcoming album *Butterfly*. As expected, Walter
Afanasieff was on board for the ballad numbers. When it came to Mariah's
music, the singer considered Walter a surrogate father. She would not think
of doing an album without him. What was not altogether surprising was
that Mariah was now reaching out to the rap community and the likes of
Sean "Puffy" Combs, Q-Tip from A Tribe Called Quest, Missy "Misde-
meanor" Elliot, Wish Bone and Krazie Bone from the group Bone Thugs-n-
Harmony, and Dru Hill to help her make magic.

Mariah was amused by the public's perception that she was suddenly
dumping the gloss and glitz of her previous albums and going off into a new
rap-oriented direction. Critics with a cynical bent saw this turn as Mariah's
way of getting back at Tommy and the whole white-bread way of making
music that she felt she had been sucked into. But far from being a decision
based on spite, Mariah felt that her tenure at the top of the charts for
nearly a decade had earned her the artistic right to express what she was

really feeling without falling back on a middle-of-the-road smoke screen. "I don't think it's that much of a departure from what I've done in the past. I don't want people to be mislead into thinking that it's an entirely new thing and that I've gone entirely left field. It's not like I went psycho and I thought I was going to be a rapper. Personally, this album is about doing whatever the hell I wanted to do."

Her defiant tone on the eve of production for *Butterfly* caused some concern in the halls of Sony. There were those who thought that her breakup with Tommy had sent their star player into a deliberate self-destructive creative slide. And while Mariah tried to continue to be diplomatic, there was more than a hint of anger on her part about being held back by the Sony powers that be, despite a multiplatinum career to this point. "In the past, people were scared to let me explore other types of music that I loved and enjoyed. They [the studio heads] saw me as having this instrument, and they wanted to get the most use out of it. There were a lot of people around me who were afraid of change. I was a valuable commodity, and they didn't want to lose that. I was encouraged to act drab because drab sells records."

However, drab definitely was not the watchword during the *Butterfly* sessions. There had been some concerns that Mariah's high-society career would not mix well with the street-oriented nature of the rap stars. But nothing could have been farther from the truth. Mariah's willingness to grow in a new musical direction and the ease with which she incorporated rap rhythms and attitudes into her uptown sound quickly earned the respect of her street collaborators. More importantly, in a world in which being real is often a question of perception, in the eyes of her new music partners, Mariah was down-to-earth. "She's straight up," recalled Missy Elliot. "She's cool, she's rap."

"Honey," the projected first single off *Butterfly*, was causing the biggest stir during the recording process. Lyrically and emotionally sexy in a way Mariah had never been before, the track made a particularly strong statement — Mariah was finding her rap roots. The song was an interesting tightrope to walk. Trip to one side and Mariah could have come off as phony and false; trip to the other and she could end up alienating those who had been enraptured by her so-called safe sound. "Puffy" Combs, who described the song as "slammin'," had been cautiously optimistic about how the two highly divergent musical worlds would mix. But by the time he finished listening to "Honey," he was a believer. Even Walter Afanasieff, who had become used to creating the music behind Mariah's quiet, reflective numbers, was caught up in the infusion of new blood in the studio, and the result was an extra coat of earthy R&B on the songs "Close My Eyes" and "Whenever You Call."

Over the years, Mariah and Walter's relationship had evolved into a legitimate friendship as well, but despite their closeness, there had never been a hint of a romantic interest by either of them. However, that closeness appeared to change when Walter began producing an up-and-coming heir to the diva throne named Samantha Cole, who was very much like Mariah in looks and music styling. Mariah began to resent the time Walter was taking away from her sessions to work on Cole's album, and she must have felt that Cole was a threat to her status as top dog in the pop world. Resentment turned to jealousy when Walter and Samantha began to date. The tension between Mariah and Walter grew, and she began to challenge openly and uncharacteristically some of Walter's creative choices in the studio. Then, one night while working on her album at the famed Hit Factory Studio, Mariah's emotions exploded. A minor disagreement over the arrangement of a song grew heated and ugly, and Mariah and Walter were soon screaming at each other. The argument spilled out of the studio and into the street where passersby reportedly heard Mariah say some nasty things about Walter dating Samantha. According to a *New York Times* report, Mariah allegedly fired Walter on the spot. The pair eventually calmed down and apologized to each other. Leslie Dart, a spokesperson for Mariah, tried to smooth things over. "He got mad and she got mad. It was simply a matter of Mariah not wanting the album to be overproduced. It had nothing to do with his romantic entanglements." But this was a side of Mariah that had not been seen before, and it was one that would not soon be forgotten by the media and the public. Mariah had long been the image of cool, and these sudden, unexpected outbursts and fits of jealousy were a sign that there was some turmoil beneath her normally cool exterior.

The consensus was that the recording of *Butterfly* was a freeing experience for Mariah, and the process was extending into other aspects of her life. Long denied the opportunity to add acting to her creative life, Mariah was now free to explore it. She began taking acting lessons, and she found that exploring another side of her creativity was an eye-opening experience. "Acting has been like this real intense therapy," said Mariah in the *Los*

Angeles Times of her introduction to acting. "I would come out of the sessions emotionally drained."

On May 30, 1997, Mariah and Tommy officially announced their separation in a low-key manner that stressed the amicability of the breakup. Tommy went into seclusion and refused comment on this next step toward the dissolution of their marriage. Mariah attempted to put a positive spin on things, citing the fact that Tommy would occasionally come by and hang out at the studio during the recording of *Butterfly* and attended social functions such as the party Mariah threw for Boyz II Men's Wayna Morris. "It was time for a new beginning in a lot of ways. There are no hard feelings. There were good and bad things in my marriage. It's called being grown up about the situation and moving on." But while she put up a brave front, in the weeks and months following the separation, Mariah was emotionally all over the place. She would be playful and upbeat one moment and raw and angry the next. The tears would come at a moment's notice, and the singer who was notoriously easy to get along with was now suddenly snappish and confrontational with even those in her inner circle who had come to know when it was time to give Mariah her space. Mariah did not ignore or try to cover up her erratic state of mind. She knew exactly what was going on — her life was becoming complicated. "It's so easy to become overwhelmed during the state I'm in right now," she confessed to *Entertainment Weekly*.

Moving on for Mariah also meant dealing with being single for the first time in four years, and she was being cautious. For the most part, her social life consisted of hanging with a closeknit group of girlfriends at each other's apartments or at dance clubs. Mariah could also occasionally be found sharing a meal and good times with Puffy and other rappers or be seen at a party in the company of male models. It was all quite innocent and incredibly chaste, but the tabloids were quick to jump on the notion of the now-very-single Mariah being out and about in the company of men. And, of course, they jumped to the wrong conclusion.

The image the newspapers continued to perpetuate was that Mariah Carey had transformed herself from Miss Goody Two-Shoes to the town slut. One New York paper ran a particularly lurid tale about the new Mariah with a headline that announced "Mariah's Sexcapades." Things got so bad that when Mariah was out on the town one night with her cousin, the next day she read that she had been spotted with a mysterious gang member.

Mariah was shocked and hurt at the accusations that she would deliberately associate with lowlifes just for cheap thrills. As she patiently explained when the press asked those insensitive questions about her love life, she was inclined to form friendships with the people she worked with, and generally speaking, she worked with men more than with women, but that did not mean that she was sleeping around. "It's just funny because I've never been out there that way, and now it's like a free-for-all, and they're making me out to be a promiscuous freak. And it's not like I need to sleep with one hundred guys to make up for lost time. If I'm with somebody, it's going to be because I love him, not because I need to go wild. With all those diseases and stuff out there, I'm certainly not trying to be in everybody's bed." And, as she proudly admitted to the French publication *France Soir*, she was, figuratively speaking, still pretty much a virgin despite her years of marriage. "In what concerns love, I'm pretty much a novice. I haven't known any man with the exception of my husband. I have less experience than a teenager."

But the outlandish rumors persisted and began to interfere with her everyday life. At one point, she was ready to close a deal on an apartment in a luxury co-op when it fell through at the last minute. Later, she discovered that other tenants in the building got together and put pressure on the building owner not to sell to her because they feared their building would become party central for rappers and gang members if Mariah moved in. "It was ridiculous," Mariah said to *Time* magazine about the incident. "There were all sorts of rumors and lies about me being the next queen of gangsta rap, which did not help."

But the reality of Mariah's bumpy reentry into the singles' scene was that much of it was her own fault, if not her own doing. Her naiveté about friends and social situations often collided with the reality of her celebrity. Mariah was attempting to meet people in an atmosphere that was totally extraordinary, and she knew it. "I came into the singles' scene with a bizarre kind of handicap," she related in a *Baltimore Sun* story. "People knew me and my music, and they automatically had a preconceived idea of who I was. It made it hard for some men to accept me for who I was." Another admitted flaw in Mariah's post-Tommy life was that she went through a period of trusting a lot of people she should not have. These were people, she has candidly admitted, who were not so much interested in being her friend as

At Puff Daddy's birthday party with The Yankees' Derek Jeter

they were in hanging out with a celebrity who could order an expensive bottle of champagne or guarantee them a good booth at an exclusive club.

While Mariah was busy defending her reputation and denying the reports of men in her life, the truth was that six months after her split with Tommy, she was, in fact, secretly dating somebody; it was New York Yankees shortstop Derek Jeter. The pair had met at a charity function and found through casual conversation that they had a lot in common. For starters, Jeter, like Mariah, came from a biracial background. Their relationship progressed swiftly from friendship to romance, and according to reports, they became lovers not too long after they met. But it would not be an easy relationship to maintain. Both had professional lives that took precedence, and in Jeter's case it often took him out of town for extended periods of time. And it was the first time either had dated another high-profile celebrity. But they reportedly were equally matched when it came to passion, and so, when they did get together, the sparks flew. Word eventually leaked out that Mariah and Derek were an item. Jeter, ever the gentleman, would say only that they were seeing each other. Mariah did not deny that they were dating but would not reveal much. All she said was, "We connected because we had similar backgrounds. He's a nice guy."

The relationship was marked by a lot of spontaneous behavior in public. Gossip columns and tabloids reported that when the Yankees were in town, Mariah and Derek were spotted regularly at late-night candlelight dinners in trendy restaurants, kissing and holding each other tight. In fact, their love match reportedly began to take its toll on Jeter's on-field performance. About the time that the couple's romance began, Jeter went into a batting slump that his fellow Yankee players blamed squarely on Mariah. They complained that she was not allowing Derek to get enough sleep, showing up at his apartment at all hours of the day and night. Word of Mariah and Derek's romance eventually got back to Tommy who was heartbroken at the news. This was a surprising change of attitude from Mottola who, in the early stages of their breakup, had been indifferent to their deteriorating relationship. He had always hoped that he and Mariah would somehow patch things up and get back together. But now he was convinced that Mariah had moved on, and so he went ahead and sold their dream home, the ten-million-dollar mansion. Mariah reportedly received half of the proceeds.

The thrill of an album she was truly proud of and the high of being in love was tempered midway through 1997 when her sister Allison announced that she was preparing to write a book that would state that her mother, Patricia, and Mariah willingly went along with her working as a prostitute, and that much of her earnings from prostitution had gone into financing Mariah's early career efforts. Mariah could do nothing but sadly deny all her sister's charges and hope that Allison somehow would straighten out her life. But, privately, she had to feel that her relationship with her sister was now permanently damaged and that reconciliation was out of the question. "Sometimes you can only give as much as you can give," she sighed during an interview with a reporter from Sweden. "You can't heal those people. A human can only heal herself."

Mariah's newfound independence in the studio was putting her in direct conflict with many of the elements of her singing career that had made her a superstar. Walter Afanasieff, in particular, was frustrated. Long used to working with Mariah on ballads with glossy and often complex pop arrangements, he was now often finding himself at odds with Mariah who wanted to take her music more in the direction of hip-hop. Walter's interpretation was a surprising contradiction to Mariah's assessment of their creative relationship. "I wanted to do so much more," Afanasieff said to *Entertainment Weekly*, "and she wanted to keep it light and rhythm and blues. She was trying to show her independence and sweetness and to let the whole corporate thing of Tommy and Sony drop off her for a while."

Midway through the sessions on *Butterfly*, Mariah took the next big step in her professional emancipation when she fired her longtime manager Randy Hoffman and attorney Alan Grubman. While both men had done an admirable job for her and the parting was reportedly amicable, they had been handpicked by Tommy Mottola, and Mariah was looking for a clean break. In a *Los Angeles Times* interview, Grubman recalled the reality of the split. "She wanted new people around her. And with the changes she's going through in her personal life, I agreed this was a wise thing." Mariah would ultimately hire Sandy Gallin as her new manager. Mariah reasoned that Gallin, with her Hollywood connections, would not only oversee her music career, but would be helpful in allowing her to make the long-hoped-for crossover into acting. She also hired a new attorney and an independent publicist. "It's been a gradual process of gaining control," said Mariah. "I've learned to be strong and independent. I've learned to trust my own judgment."

Around this time, Mariah stepped up her acting plans when she entered into a deal with Touchstone Pictures to produce and star in a film entitled *All that Glitters*, a story about an eighties singer who triumphs over all odds to become a superstar. It was a story that Mariah insisted would not be autobiographical even though it felt that way.

And for Mariah, her coming-of-age as an independent woman could not have come at a better time for her and a worst time for her label, Columbia-Sony. Despite having world superstars such as Oasis and Céline Dion on its roster, the company was showing signs of falling from the top-five list in terms of total sales. The consensus among music-industry journalists was that the only thing keeping the label afloat was the consistent sales of Mariah Carey, whose records routinely sold in the millions. But with her separation from Sony president Tommy Mottola and their impending divorce on the horizon, as well as the fact that Mariah had only two albums left on her contract with Sony, there was real tension in the corporate hallways. The question was on everybody's lips: would Mariah resign from the label when her obligations were over? Mariah was in the driver's seat, and she knew it. If she walked, there would no doubt be a bidding war to end all bidding wars among record companies, and from a purely financial point of view, she would come out on top. Many outsiders thought that Mariah leaving Sony and letting the company go down the tubes would be the ultimate revenge against Tommy. But while Mariah had not made any decision about leaving at that point, she was, in fact, leaning toward staying. "If I were to leave the company, it would in effect be saying that my relationship with Tommy was the only reason for my being there, and that's not true. There are thousands of people at Sony who kill for my music, and I'm looking forward to continuing with them."

In the midst of recording *Butterfly*, Mariah was once again faced with having to drop everything to deal with yet another lawsuit from a disgruntled songwriter who was claiming she ripped him off. This time it was a struggling songwriter and former bodyguard for seventies funk star Sly Stone, named Christopher Siletti, who claimed that the song "Hero," on the 1993 album *Music Box*, had plagiarized one of his songs. The resulting trial dragged on for two months before a judge dismissed the lawsuit. Mariah was growing weary of these court battles and false charges but had resigned herself to the fact that they were part of the price she had to pay for success.

Mariah finished *Butterfly* in August 1997 and began the usual round of prerelease hype. Mariah was genuinely excited at the prospect of promoting this album, she considered to be a new beginning for her. "This album is definitely something I've wanted to do for a long time," she told *Jet*. "It's been a gradual process of my being able to say that this is what I'm going to do at this point. People owe it to you to let you express yourself." And it was during this round of interviews that the singer acknowledged that, for the first time, she was doing a different kind of music. "This was more of a big-city record," she told a Swedish interviewer. "This time, I could work with the hip-hop artists I wanted to work with."

Any fears that this new direction for Mariah might put off longtime fans were brushed aside on September 13, 1997 when the single "Honey" was released and immediately went to number one on the *Billboard* charts. Three days later, *Butterfly* also made its debut at number one. *Butterfly* was Mariah Carey's coming-of-age album. The creative rush of being out from under the control of her husband and record producers and the critical acceptance of *Daydream* had given Mariah the confidence to delve deeper into the hip-hop world. The hugely autobiographical "Honey" and the down-and-dirty "Breakdown" and "Babydoll," earthy R&B tunes with a subtle hip-hop twist, are easily the most striking statements on the album. A bit farther down the register, "The Roof" and "Shook Ones" were sly and sexy outings that portrayed Mariah as a new woman capable of unexpected passions. There was also a token aside to the old Mariah in the lush ballad "Fourth of July" to let listeners know that the singer had not forgotten her roots. *Butterfly* was very much a giant creative step forward. A sure sign that Mariah had moved beyond the wreckage of her marriage was the heartfelt thank you to Tommy that appeared on the album cover's liner notes.

Critically, *Butterfly* was applauded for the chances Mariah had taken, and while the reviews were not across-the-board raves, the indication was that Mariah's new musical strides were reaching a responsive audience. Her hard work and perseverance were rewarded with a slew of award nominations for *Butterfly*. She captured a nomination for Best Female Artist in the R&B category from the American Music Awards. The Blockbuster Entertainment Awards nominated her for Favorite Female in the pop-music category. Even her recent Grammy drought ended with three nominations: Best Female Vocal Performer, Best Female R&B Vocal Performer, and Best R&B Song.

Mariah plunged full bore into a variety of promotional appearances that seemed to indicate the singer had finally come out of her shell. She appeared, with her mother, on *The Oprah Winfrey Show*. That was a painful experience as Oprah probed the personal side of her life and led Mariah to shed tears several times during the hour. Mariah appeared for an autograph signing at Tower Records in New York, grateful for the rare opportunity to meet her fans face-to-face. Mariah also appeared on *Saturday Night Live* a second time and captivated millions of television viewers with powerful renditions of the songs "Butterfly" and "My All."

Mariah's growing popularity as a worldwide star led to requests for more concerts. And while *Butterfly* was burning up the charts and radio airwaves, Mariah chose to once again kick off her current round of concert tours with a series of concerts in Japan, Australia, and Hawaii and went into active rehearsal for the tour shortly before Christmas. Mariah kicked off the first of twelve concert dates — her longest concert tour to date — on January 11 with four sold-out dates in Tokyo. Echoing her U.S. tour, Mariah's first show in Tokyo was not her best, and her nerves once again betrayed her onstage. But just like the U.S. tour, she made a quick recovery, and those who saw the remaining Tokyo shows deemed them a rousing success. A quick trip across the water for a concert in Taiwan was followed by a series of six shows in Australia. A final show in Hawaii ended the tour on a high note.

During the tour, Mariah found out that once again, she was shut out from the Grammy Awards — not one of her three nominations had won. But this time, she took it all in stride. She was on tour, the fans loved her, and at least she didn't have to sit through the whole awards ceremony and then come away empty-handed. No amount of awards could replace the popular acceptance of *Butterfly* and the feeling that she was now free to live her own life — creatively and personally. In fact, it was that feeling, coupled with the fact that her relationship with Derek Jeter was going well, that brought her to the decision, in March 1998, that it was time to divorce Tommy Mottola. A trip to the Dominican Republic and a quickie uncontested divorce put the official stamp on her new life. Mariah returned to the United States a free woman and, that same day, was in the stands watching as Derek Jeter had a less-than-stellar game, striking out twice. This just added more fuel to the theory that Mariah's loving was bad for Derek's game.

The closing of the door on the Tommy Mottola chapter of her life was more than counterbalanced by the doors that continued to open professionally. One of the most enticing was her participation in the two-hour concert television special *VH-1 Divas Live!*, featuring Mariah solo and in concert with Céline Dion, Gloria Estafan, Shania Twain, Aretha Franklin, and Carole King. The coming together of these superstars was an egoless experience in which the women created a flawless series of dynamic performances. The concert aired on May 21 to huge ratings and great reviews. She continued to moonlight on other artists' albums, and many of these choices reflected her wide-ranging musical interests. She sang on the song "Sweetheart" on the album by JD, duetted with the group The League on the song "Freestyle Pt. 2" on the album *Funkmaster Flex Vol. III*, and sang with Patti Labelle on "Got to Be Real" on the album *Patti Labelle: Live! One Night Only*.

However, the good times were still being roughed up by the constant intrusion of accusations into Mariah's personal life. This took a particularly ugly turn in June 1998 when a New Jersey limo driver named Franco D'Onofrio filed a $1.5 million-dollar lawsuit against her, charging that he had been unlawfully fired from his job as her personal driver after four years and that she owed the limousine company forty thousand dollars in unpaid bills. D'Onofrio also claimed that during his tenure as her driver, he had driven Mariah to numerous romantic rendezvous with Derek Jeter as early as 1996, when Mariah was still married to Tommy. Mariah immediately filed a countersuit, charging that the unpaid bills amounted to no more than five thousand dollars, and that his stories were lies. The suit was eventually settled in Mariah's favor, but the damage done to her reputation and relationship with Jeter was something that would not go away.

The press simply would not let go of the Mariah–Derek romance. New York papers were particularly intrusive, speculating that the couple were already engaged, and that a wedding date was imminent. The specter of Allison Carey resurfaced in these reports when they claimed that Mariah's sister's long-threatened book would state, among other things, that Mariah and Derek were already secretly dating in 1996, an accusation that Mariah had thought was resolved with the D'Onofrio suit. Derek responded by saying, "I'm not engaged. I'm not getting married." Mariah angrily added, "There is no engagement. There is no ring." And while they continued to deny the allegations, the reality was that Derek and Mariah's love affair was dissolving without the help of any outside media interference. Time apart was putting a constant strain on their relationship, and when it was all said and done, their love was not enough to keep them together. Mariah's spokesperson put the cold, final note on the relationship when she said, "Media pressure was too much for them as a couple, and they are now just good friends."

In his autobiography published in 2000, Derek Jeter spoke about their romance. "I learned that it would be very difficult to seriously date a high-profile person. I wasn't used to getting a lot of attention because I went to dinner with someone. It turned my life into a more chaotic existence than I wanted." By mid-1998, the pair had split up. Mariah was strong in the wake of the breakup, but there was a touch of sadness as well. "It just didn't work out," she said. "But there was life for a minute."

CHAPTER TEN

Happily...

Mariah recovered rather quickly from her first post-divorce romance, or so it appeared on the surface. Friends and close personal associates noticed that while she was not exactly withdrawn, Mariah was a little quieter than she had been when she was in love. "Derek" was no longer the first thing that tumbled out of her mouth, and she was not anxious to dissect the failed relationship. Her friends felt that she would survive it and move on, but like everything else, it would take time.

Once again, there were the rumors. The affair with Derek Jeter had reportedly hit Mariah so hard that she had allegedly told close friends she had given up on ever finding true love again. There were even some truly incredible reports that she was considering going back to Tommy. As always, reality fell somewhere in the middle. She had been hurt but not devastated, and it was a hurt mixed with large measures of simple disappointment. And while she would laugh off the notion that she would never love again, she was cautious, in idle conversation, in describing what kind of person she could fall in love with. It was a given that she could not love anybody who was not her equal financially and professionally. This may sound a bit un-Mariahlike, but the singer was aware of certain realities, and one of the biggest was that in order to be taken care of emotionally, any would-be romance would have to measure up in her material world as well. Of course, that did not necessarily mean that true love did not exist outside the music business. At the end of the day, Mariah knew that all she needed was love and respect and perhaps someone to take care of her.

Mariah and Whitney Houston record "When You Believe"
SUPPLIED BY GLOBE PHOTOS

She was sure that person was out there waiting for her — somewhere. Because, despite the rough patches, Mariah still believed in fairy tales and happy endings.

In years gone by, the first sign of stress drove Mariah racing back to the security of the recording studio to begin work on her next studio album. Psychologically, it had always worked for Mariah to squirrel herself away from the pain. Now, when she did make occasional forays into the studio, it didn't have the same effect. She would admit that it was more of a mind exercise and she was less inclined toward anything definite. At this point in her career, she felt that it would be counterproductive to consider recording an album unless she was in a positive state of mind. So, the studio was on hold for now, but with her newfound freedom, other opportunities began to present themselves.

Her association with Disney's Touchstone Pictures on the still-in-development *All That Glitters* had put her in touch with the people who were putting together the soundtrack for their latest animated movie *The Lion King*. Mariah was thrilled when she was asked to sing "When You Believe," a song in which Whitney Houston had already expressed an interest. But Disney executives' suggestion that Mariah and Whitney sing in duet on the song was even more intriguing to Mariah. For years, the press had painted Mariah as heir apparent to Whitney's title of Queen of the Divas and, in the process, had built up a nonexistent rivalry between the pair with reports that the two singers would often fuel this conflict with alleged snide put-downs. The reality was that no such animosity existed as far as the two singers was concerned, and doing the song would give them the opportunity to clear the air.

The recording of "When You Believe" turned out to be a joyous occasion for Mariah. She and Whitney immediately bonded, and the session that resulted in "When You Believe" was often punctuated by laughs and the kind of conversations only good friends have. Whitney agreed that "Mariah and I had good chemistry together." Added Mariah in an MTV interview, "If we were ever going to come together on any kind of record, this is definitely the right one, and really the coolest thing to me is all the drama and everybody making it like we had a rivalry. She was just really cool, and we had a really good time in the studio. We had fun."

Mariah's growing interest in acting had reached a point where she and her teacher felt that she was ready to test the waters. "She's committed to learning another craft," said her acting teacher Sheila Gray in *Elle* magazine. "She's willing to take a chance. I think that's courageous." So the superstar set forth into uncharted waters and started to make the rounds of auditions. Mariah was cautious and realistic in approaching Hollywood. Her name would get her in the door, but only her skills would land her the role. She knew there would be those who would try to use her in an exploitive way, and she knew that she was far from a polished actress. The movie business would have to work on her terms.

From the outset, Mariah met with encouragement from the film community. Casting agents would often comment on how she came across as a real person and that for somebody with no acting experience to speak of, she could easily slip into a wide variety of emotions at the drop of a hat. One of the first roles she auditioned for was as the love interest for Chris Tucker in the James Bond comedy spoof *Double O Soul*. But, as often happens in Hollywood, the film ran into numerous production delays that precluded Mariah's involvement.

During this period, Mariah was once again entertaining the idea of a full-blown U.S. tour. For her, the performing jitters were definitely gone, as witness her August performance at radio station KMEL's All Star Jam in San Francisco. But the reality was that if she were to tour, any recording plans would have to be put on hold, and she had to be ready to drop everything at a moment's notice if *All That Glitters* suddenly got back on track.

With *Butterfly* continuing to show a steady chart presence and its sales heading toward five million copies — ultimately reaching a total of ten million — there really was no rush to put out another studio album. But with the lucrative holiday season coming Sony was wringing their collective hands at the possibility of having no Mariah Carey album in stores for the first time in nearly a decade. The answer seemed simple. Mariah had a total of thirteen number-one hits in her career, more than enough to fill a greatest-hits album. And greatest-hits albums by topselling artists had become something of a Christmas tradition and were usually money in the bank as well as a guaranteed chart fix. But Mariah felt that simply releasing a greatest-hits package was like preaching to the converted and believed her fans should be rewarded for their support with something new as well. She couldn't spare the time to produce a whole new album from scratch, so a compromise was reached. The greatest-hits album, *Ones*, would also contain four new songs. The bonus tracks would include "When You Believe," her duet with Whitney Houston, another duet, this one with singer Brian McKnight, "Whenever You Call," and two Mariah solo songs, "I Still Believe" and "Sweetheart." "It's not really a greatest-hits album," Mariah told MTV. "I've only been around less than ten years. It's really only the number one songs I've had. If it were truly a greatest-hits package, it would contain some other songs that did not make it to number one." Still, the process of recording the new songs and once again working with a lot of different people was just what Mariah needed. It gave her the opportunity to exercise her talents without having to deal with any undue pressure.

Given her continued status as "the franchise" for Sony, it came as a shock, midway through 1998, when Sony announced that Mariah's Crave label had been dissolved. Mariah was disappointed and relieved at the same time. Being involved with developing new artists and working with them in the studio had been a joy, but dealing with the endless rounds of paperwork and the corporate bottom line had not. During its one year of existence, Crave had produced one top-ten single — "Head Over Heels" by the group Allure — and its other acts had shown across-the-board promise more than enough to justify Crave's survival. So, what happened? The press reported that the end of Crave was caused by a combination of financial considerations and Mariah's loss of interest in the day-to-day work required to run a label. The rumor-mongers immediately jumped on Crave's end as a not-too-subtle act of revenge against Mariah in the aftermath of her divorce from Tommy. Mariah did not want to believe that was the case, but she confessed in *Launch* magazine, "My situation with Sony is far more unique and complex because of the personal aspect of what it used to be."

But Mariah's disappointment with the end of Crave was shortlived as the November 1998 release of *Ones* indicated that her name still carried strength with music buyers. Despite being essentially a greatest-hits package, *Ones* quickly rose to number four on the album charts and, in the ensuing months, would quietly go triple platinum. The consensus among the music press was that Mariah's insistence on including the new material made all the difference in increasing sales figures more than expected. Including some new with the old in a greatest-hits package had been tried from time to time by other artists with varying degrees of success, but with the triumph of *Ones*, it would become a regular element in nearly all future greatest-hits albums. As such packages go, *Ones* was a solid retrospective of Mariah's chart hits, but because these songs were oversaturating the radio, including a favorite nonhit album track or two might have made a nice change. The new songs were a definite bonus even though none ever really rose to the spectacular level of her best. And while some would occasionally make appearances in Mariah's live shows, collectively, they added up to a nice touch but little more.

As 1998 began to wind down, Mariah felt at ease, so much so that she decided to take the month of December off to spend some quiet vacation time on the slopes of Aspen, Colorado. Aspen had long ago become the getaway of choice for the superstars of the entertainment industry, and since celebrity sightings are considered part of the scenery, the stars are pretty much left alone. Mariah wanted to be ignored for a while. This was the kind of get-away-from-it-all Christmas she was yearning for. The real-estate agent who rented Mariah her Aspen retreat was a big fan. What Mariah was unaware of was that her agent had a friend who had, coincidentally, rented a house to Latino singing sensation Luis Miguel, and that they had decided to moonlight as matchmakers. Mariah's agent told her that Luis was in town and wanted to meet her. Miguel's agent told Luis that Mariah was interested in meeting him. "Of course, they both kind of lied,"

Cuddling with Luis Miguel

laughed Mariah. Mariah hesitated. She was a bit unsure. After all, she came to Aspen looking for solitude, not a date. But she decided that with the relative anonymity Aspen accorded her, it couldn't hurt to meet Miguel. She was, in fact, a fan of his music. So, unless he turned out to be a complete nincompoop, they would have something to talk about. Free and easy was what she had in mind. The pair got together the day before Christmas Eve. It was love at first sight.

Mariah admitted that she did not know where the relationship was heading during those first few days. Neither did Luis. The Latin singer had recently ended a long-term relationship with actress Daisy Fuentes and was gun-shy about getting romantically involved again. But both would later admit that something magic passed between them on the day they met. For Mariah and Luis, even the most mundane moments were the greatest things on earth. They were together constantly, and the intimacy and romance followed quickly. On Christmas Eve, Luis presented Mariah with a diamond necklace. But Mariah would later state that while the pure emotion of love washed over them, there were certain realities that instantly bound the two together. Their personalities meshed. Luis was a totally optimistic person and free with his attentions. And most important, he was not the controlling type, which fit perfectly with Mariah's insistence on having her freedom.

"Since Luis Miguel came into my life, I am a much more happy person," she cooed in *Gente* magazine. "He's a very self-confident person. That's what I like about him. At this moment in my life, I'm so happy with the relationship. We have a lot in common. We both understand the pressures and the time you have to dedicate to this job." Which was why, the same month they met, Mariah was not too upset when Luis had to jet off to the other side of the world for a series of concerts. Mariah was in love, but she was also cautious. She conceded that the whirlwind romance could have been a result of rampant emotion that could well have burned itself out. But, in the coming months, when the gifts, phone calls, and visits continued, Mariah knew this love was for real. "I used to have this dream when I was a little girl that someday I would meet somebody who was mixed race like me and who had a similar life, and that we would live happily ever after, and that he would complete me," she told *Rolling Stone*.

Mariah continued to set her sights on acting roles and, when her starring vehicle *All That Glitters* was once again delayed, she went after other parts. She auditioned for the role of Natasha in the live-action film *The Adventures of Rocky and Bullwinkle*. She came close to landing it but ultimately lost to Rene Russo. Then she was rewarded with her first part when she won the role of Chris O'Donnell's ex-girlfriend in the romantic comedy *The Bachelor*, which would begin filming shortly after the New Year. *The Bachelor* was an eye-opening experience for Mariah. It was only one day of filming, but it proved to be a strenuous one. Mariah played an opera singer in a scene that called for her to sing a rousing aria from the opera *La Traviata* before suddenly falling over dead. "It was totally over the top," recalled Mariah in a *Mirabella* magazine interview. "The director said, 'Okay you need a stunt double for that fall, right?' And I said, 'Nah, I can do that', not realizing I was going to have to do thirty more takes. By the end of shooting, my hips and knees were killing me, and a medic had to bring me ice."

When she was not working, Mariah would hop a plane and jet off to be wherever Luis happened to be, which often meant far-flung locations such as Paris and Mexico City where the pair would be spotted holding hands and kissing in restaurants and other public places. Initially the couple had attempted to keep their relationship out of the public eye, but now, confident that their love was real, they made no attempt to hide their feelings. And for Mariah, the sensation proved liberating. She was tired of hiding her love affairs in dark corners and dodging the prying eye of the press. If she had taken nothing else away from her relationship with Derek Jeter, it was that she was not going to hide any future love affairs.

Given Mariah's state of romantic bliss, it was surprising that in May 1999, an old jealousy would once again surface. It involved Samantha Cole (Walter Afanasieff's one-time girlfriend) and a very public display of Mariah's temperament. Mariah and a group of friends were partying at an exclusive New York nightclub when Samantha Cole walked in. According to eyewitness reports, chronicled in the *New York Daily News*, Mariah began chucking pieces of ice across the room at the singer. When that did not persuade her to leave, Mariah reportedly went to the bouncers in an attempt to get her removed from the club. Mariah and her spokespeople were mum on this incident, but Samantha had plenty to say: "She [Mariah] is always talking about me. I regret that we can't be friends. There's room for ten more pop divas out there."

Following the completion of *The Bachelor*, Mariah turned her attention back to *All That Glitters*, which was once again green-lighted. Part of the deal was for Mariah to compose the songs and music for the film, and so she immediately settled back into the studio. Drawing on her own life for the fictional story, Mariah had soon fashioned several songs that reflected moody, emotional highs and lows but, in keeping with the seting of the movie, with a definite eighties feel. At the rate she was going, Mariah felt that the soundtrack would be completed just before she stepped in front of the cameras. Unfortunately, *All That Glitters* start time was pushed back yet again, and so Mariah was once more left in limbo with a handful of songs. "I was like 'okay'," she told the *Baltimore Sun*. "If I'm going to do this, I'm either going to use some of the songs from the soundtrack or go back to square one and do a completely different album. So I decided to take the songs I had already done and just do a completely different album."

Sony was delighted at the news that they would get a new Mariah Carey album in 1999. Once again, they were less than thrilled when Mariah announced that she would be recruiting such rap and hip-hop stars as Jay-Z, Snoop Dogg, Da Brat, and Missy Elliot to help her make further inroads into rap and R&B. Although never made public, many in the Sony Records corporate empire believed that Mariah had worked the experimentation out of her system with *Butterfly*, and that she would now return to safe and potentially more lucrative middle-of-the-road pop. But with her newfound sense of independence, Mariah was having none of that. "It's a challenge to work with other artists," she told *Breakout* magazine. "On my first four albums, there were no songs with other artists because I was not allowed to. But, now that I decide what I do, I ask everybody to join in on my records." For *Rainbow*, Mariah also made the decision to record in Capri, Italy rather than her normal recording haunts in New York. Part of the reason was personal. Luis was currently on tour in Europe, and by recording in Italy, it made it easier for the couple to get together for some private time. But business also figured into the equation. "I love New York," she told a *Blitz TV* interviewer. "But if I'm there, I want to go out, friends come to the studio, and the phone rings constantly. But in Capri, I am in a remote place, and there is no one I can run into."

Mariah immediately rang up Walter Afanasieff who was integral to creating her trademark ballads. Unfortunately, Afanasieff, who had become an in-house producer for other Sony acts largely because of his work with

Mariah, was busy working on another album and was not available. Mariah was disappointed and just a little bit suspicious. Again, she speculated that the fact that Walter was not available for her new album was Sony's doing; it was another stumbling block put in her path because of lingering hard feelings resulting from her divorce from Tommy. The falling out between Walter and Mariah appeared to be due to creative differences and not just to Sony's interference, but the record company's insistence on not respond-ing to the rumors only fueled suspicions that they were interfering with Mariah as some kind of revenge for her breakup with Tommy.

But she was not going to let the absence of Walter derail the album. David Foster had a reputation as a producer who knew his way around a ballad and who had a keen commercial sense. He was available and anxious at the opportunity to work with Mariah. For the album's dance-rap hip-hop songs, which she felt would end up taking up at least half of the album, she chose the solid-gold hip-hop-rap producers Jimmy Jam and Terry Lewis. While she talked up Jam and Lewis to *Launch* magazine, Mariah, uncharac-teristically, took the opportunity to take a shot at Walter. "I think Jimmy and Terry have added a different direction musically. I told them how great it was to be able to sit there (in the studio) and not have to say 'No. Not so schmaltzy.'"

As she had with *Butterfly*, Mariah was going for an eclectic mix of styles and sounds. One of the more adventurous steps was a R&B-laced pop-ballad remake of the Phil Collins hit "Against All Odds (Take a Look at Me Now)." Mariah's respect for Collins's original was such that she re-corded a demo and had it shipped directly to him to get his opinion. She added it to the album's playlist only when Collins wired back his okay on what she had done. At the suggestion of Foster, Mariah also brought in songwriter Diane Warren to help her hammer out the lyrics for two ballads, "Can't Take that Away" and "After Tonight." Warren, who had written for Joe Cocker and Aerosmith, among others, would later recall that there had been a strong give-and-take relationship in the writing sessions with Mariah. She mentioned that Mariah would often stop her in mid-lyric to say that what she was writing did not work for her and demand something better. But she was also quick to accept the Warren contributions when they did work. Mariah was particularly happy with "After Tonight," feeling that the lyrics spoke very much to her real-life relationship with Luis Miguel. She felt that the song would work perfectly as a duet, and that she and Luis singing together would be ideal musically as well as romantically. But according to David Foster who supervised the sessions on "After To-night," the experiment in love and song was a total disaster. "The song had been written just for Mariah," the producer stated in a *New York Daily News* article. "I had Luis and Mariah record the song as a duet several times. But it never really sounded right." Mariah painfully recalled the failed experiment. "'After Tonight' just wasn't in Luis's key. To change it, I would have had to redo my vocals, and we just didn't have the time."

The failed recording made for some tense moments in the studio be-tween Mariah and Luis. After hearing the recording later, Luis reportedly became so upset that he cut the tape up into pieces and mailed it back to David Foster. But that incident aside, Luis's visits to Capri during the re-cording of *Rainbow*, were a tranquil and positive time for Mariah who was in a cocoon of love and good feeling as she recorded the album. There were those days when Mariah and Luis would walk hand-in-hand through the market shopping stalls or sit for hours in local outdoor restaurants. "Yes, I am in love," she cautiously explained to *Caras* magazine, still weighing the need to keep things private. "I don't want to give details about my private life. I'm living in a very nice period after having really bad and stormy years."

Even when Luis was not around, Mariah was enjoying the spartan ex-istence while recording the album. Capri was a hilly island, which meant that Mariah had to walk everywhere. For a while, Mariah would make the long daily trek up a steep hillside to the recording studio. But after a time, that daily climb took its toll physically, and so she began to sleep in the studio. Mariah quickly settled into a routine. When Luis was not around, she would wake up, sing in the studio until her voice gave out, and then go back to sleep. In the studio, Mariah was hands-on despite the presence of first-rate producers, and she won the respect of the other music-makers. The *Rainbow* sessions, even more than those for *Butterfly*, were turning out to be cathartic and, to a large extent, biographical. The song "Heart-breaker," which had its inception in the *All That Glitters* era, was a mirror on Mariah's life played out against a backdrop of different musical styles and emotional lyrics. Even before the sessions ended, "Heartbreaker" was the odds-on favorite to be the first single. Here was yet another tune that seemed to reflect where Mariah had been and where she was going.

Mariah had a long and diverse history of involvement with charitable causes. In the early nineties, she became involved in The Fresh Air Fund, which took underprivileged New York kids to summer camps in the country in an attempt to let them see a different world. Her other generous involvements include working with the New York Police Athletic League and working for the benefit of the obstetrics department of New York Hospital — Cornell Medical Center. "I try to be a good person and make a difference where I can, in the world and with people," Mariah said. Her list of charity causes increased once again during the recording of *Rainbow* when famed opera singer Luciano Pavarotti asked her to the perform, along with such stellar celebrities as Ricky Martin, Michael Jackson, B.B. King, and Joe Cocker, at a charity concert in nearby Modena, Italy on June 1. Mariah jumped at the chance to perform in front of an Italian audience for the first time and, by all reports, put on an electrifying show. A CD of that show, entitled *Pavarotti and Friends*, would be released in September and featured Mariah and Pavarotti duetting on the song "Hero" and her live rendition of "My All."

By the end of summer 1999, Mariah had completed *Rainbow* in what was for her the record time of three months. She turned over the master tapes to Sony and waited for the expected gasps at the fact that *Rainbow* had taken an even bigger step in the direction of the street. But rather than let the potential negative reaction of the execs to the notion that she was jumping on the rap-hip-hop bandwagon bother her, Mariah was amused. "People just don't understand," she chuckled in a *Newsweek* interview. "I grew up with this music."

Once again Mariah plunged into the promotion stream, making the expected television appearances and the rounds of the magazine, newspaper, and radio journalists. Mariah was, for the first time, totally at ease with the media. She anticipated and was prepared for the questions about Tommy and Luis, as well as the tabloid reports, and she handled them all with style and grace. What was encouraging was that the press was interested in her music and the direction it was taking. But, most of all, Mariah came away from this latest bout with the media with the feeling that she was finally getting a measure of respect. In an interview with MTV, she indicated that getting respect has never been easy for her. "People look at me and think 'Oh, she sings all the octaves and does all that stuff' and they don't acknowledge that the stuff I do is really my own style and my own thing."

Mariah Volunteering for the New York Police Athletic Association
ED GELLER / GLOBE PHOTOS

"Heartbreaker" was released in September and debuted at a respectable number sixteen on the singles charts, but it would not stay there long. Audiences instantly embraced Mariah's further musical adventures into the world of hip-hop and rhythm and blues. Within a week, the single leaped to number one. By the time "Heartbreaker" hit the top spot, Mariah was winging her way to Spain for a promotional tour before the November 2 release of *Rainbow*. The U.S. release of the album was shaping up to be a media event of major proportions, complete with a battle of the television morning news shows. The new CBS television show *The Early Show* had the inside track on Mariah, premiering her new album live in a miniconcert on November 1. But at the last minute, the producers of *The Early Show* had trouble getting the appropriate permits for the show. NBC's *The Today Show* stepped in at the last possible moment, and so Mariah, on the appointed day, wowed a crowd outside *The Today Show* studios.

Rainbow raced up the album charts to number two amid a tidal wave of solid reviews that emphasized Mariah's new musical direction. These comments brought a smile to Mariah's face when she explained that what she was doing now was an extension of her love for the music of the street that has always been with her. But there were some brickbats aimed in the direction of Mariah's album. It was intimated that many of the songs on *Rainbow* sounded alike. Mariah was quick to dismiss the charges, citing the way she wrote her songs and saying that if her fans liked her music, she couldn't care less about what the critics said.

Rainbow was the clean break Mariah had been looking for. Although there were gestures towards the types of songs that had made her a star, the mixing of tougher sounding R&B and hip-hop elements was even more brazen. "Heartbreaker" was the real eye-opening track, with its lyrical musings about lost love set to a slow, driving beat. "Crybaby" with the nongangsta stylings of Snoop Dogg, was also an earthy indication that Mariah's sweet-sounding vocals could mix effectively with just about any style. Easily as daring in concept and execution as *Butterfly*, *Rainbow* effectively announced the next phase of Mariah Carey's career. Along with the accolades for *Rainbow* came the inevitable round of statistics that gave her the highly rarefied status of superstar. By the time the dust settled on *Rainbow*, Mariah's worldwide sales in the nineties had surpassed 120 million copies. Her string of consecutive number-one chart singles had put her in the company of The Beatles and Elvis, among others.

Mariah took an extended vacation during the remainder of 1999. She would spend a lot of time in Europe with Luis, often watching backstage at his concerts as thousands of young women went crazy for her man. Of course, there were also those quiet times when the love of Mariah and Luis deepened. There were the inevitable tabloid reports of possible marriage and alleged plans for Mariah to begin having children. Mariah and Luis would laugh off these reports. There would be time for those things later when they were ready. But for now, they rejoiced in what they had.

Unfortunately, during this period, Mariah's sister Allison made good on her threat to expose the alleged truth about her relationship with Mariah when she announced on an English website that she had published a book called *Mariah and Me*, which, according to alleged excerpts, chronicled in detail how Allison supported Mariah through prostitution prior to her landing a record deal and that she had actually rented the limo and bought Mariah a new dress for her initial meeting with Tommy Mottola. Allison also stated that Mariah had unsuccessfully threatened and attempted to bribe her to keep the book from being published. Although Allison has

said that the manuscript is completed, to date, the book has not been published, and it appears that she had only been releasing portions of the
manuscript in an attempt to interest a publisher. Allison is still struggling
with her demons. Through her spokesperson, Mariah issued a statement
that said "Mariah has supported her sister since she made her first album
and continues to support her children. Any illicit activities her sister engaged in were for her own means. The woman has been in and out of re-
hab and treatment centers. It's a sad situation."

Mariah returned to the States in mid-November to tape a labor of love,
the television show *Mariah Carey's Homecoming Special*, which would be
filmed in the gymnasium of her old junior high school. For Mariah, this was a
mixed blessing. She reveled in the nostalgia of it all as she hugged and
kissed a number of her old teachers and principals and accepted their
praise. But the memories of these people trying to dissuade her from her
dream as a young girl were also on her mind. It would have been easy to
rub their noses in her success. But that was not her style. The show was a
success, and the consensus was that Mariah was truly giving it a little bit
extra. *The Mariah Carey Homecoming Special* aired on the Fox Channel
on December 14. Mariah received another Christmas present in early December when Disney once again announced that the off-again-on-again *All
That Glitters* was a go and was looking at a year 2000 start date, pointing
toward a hopeful Christmas 2000 release.

The door to Mariah Carey's past life literally and figuratively closed in
mid-December when the mansion she had shared with Tommy Mottola
burned to the ground in what authorities termed an accidental fire. Tommy
had already sold their dream home, but the memories were still there.
Mariah was sad at the news but also managed a wan smile at the symbol-
ism of it all. It was also during this period that she began to hear stories
about how her ex had got on with his life and was actively dating. Mariah
was happy for him.

Christmas and New Year's was a whirlwind of activity for Mariah. She
spent some time with her family and some time globe-trotting with Luis.
She entered the year 2000 in a very good place. And she was once again
ready to tour.

CHAPTER ELEVEN

... Ever After

Despite her phenomenal sales in the United States and a number of well-received television specials, Mariah was feeling a bit guilty about the fact that she had not toured her native country since 1993 and had, in fact, performed more live shows in Europe and Asia than she ever had in her place of birth. Now, she reasoned, was the time for payback. Actually, there was a lot in it for Mariah herself to tour at this time. Her confidence as a performer had grown considerably since 1993, and she felt U.S. audiences would see her at her best, which was important to her. And being particularly proud of *Rainbow*, she was anxious to give Americans first shot at hearing the new songs live. Plus, for the first time in a long time, she did not feel an overwhelming urge to go back into the studio. The tour would consist of nine North American concerts, with stops in Los Angeles, Las Vegas, Dallas, Chicago, Miami, Atlanta, Boston, Toronto, and New York. Mariah hinted that, since her live show would cover much of the material from *Rainbow*, it should not be too much of a surprise if some of the artists who helped out on the album happened to show up to be a part of her upcoming concert dates. On March 3, ten days before the tour was set to commence in Los Angeles, singer and good buddy Da Brat signed on as Mariah's opening act.

These were heady times for Mariah as she went through the rehearsals for the upcoming tour. She was hearing much of the *Rainbow* material in its completed form for the first time outside the studio, and she was thrilled at the prospect of her new direction translating well in a concert setting. Going back to the selection of songs from older albums was like revisiting old friends. And while she felt duty-bound to present her greatest hits in the familiar way that her fans had come to know them, she was not above tweaking the arrangements or bringing her vocals down an octave or two in an attempt to give them fresh life and feeling. By the time the rehearsals were completed, Mariah felt confident that the show she would take on her march through the states would be a blockbuster.

The buzz among music-industry pundits was that a Mariah Carey concert tour of any duration was just the shot in the arm the whole performing industry needed. Overall, the last couple of years had been soft, with only a handful of superstar acts able to mount long, profitable tours. In fact, many acts, including the once powerhouse rockers Van Halen, had found themselves playing to half-empty houses. But a Mariah Carey tour was a whole different animal. She got out of the studio so rarely that anytime she ventured on a stage was considered an event, and, as befitting most events, Mariah's shows sold out in a matter of days. Likewise, the media was all over this tour, probing for details and scrambling for even the slightest bit of information. Again, Mariah was vague, promising a wonderful show but not wanting to spoil any surprises she might have up her sleeve.

The opening night of her tour was a full-blown Hollywood extravaganza. The stage was full of lights, costumes, fancy backdrops, and, most important, Mariah — her voice taking electrifying flight over a wide array of music that traced her career highlights throughout the nineties but with a generous sampling of the songs from *Rainbow* as well. Mariah took obvious delight in strutting her new sound before the audience, along with her new sultry, sexy persona. Between songs, she was sincere in thanking the audience for their response and acceptance. The reviews for that first show were mostly positive and near-raves, which announced that Mariah had arrived as a dynamic performer and as the consummate singer of songs. To Mariah, those reviews, after the audience's applause, were the sweetest music of all.

Mariah's tour moved east, chalking up more sold-out shows and rave reviews in Las Vegas, Dallas, Chicago, and Miami. A plus in having Mariah on the road was that the buzz inherent to these rare live appearances helped the already-massive sales of *Rainbow* jump to nearly four million copies. The follow-up single to "Heartbreaker," was a version of "Thank God I Found You," recorded with the boy group 98 Degrees. It was rocketing up the charts. And her record company was happy to report that sales of her extensive back catalog were increasing as well. The irony was that while she had never really gone away, now, suddenly, Mariah was "back."

That was why Mariah was in such a celebratory mood on the day of her Atlanta concert when she took a group of her tour mates out to dinner in an exquisite seafood restaurant. Mariah had one of her favorite dishes: oysters on the half shell. Hours later, Mariah suddenly fell ill. She was throwing up and suffering terrible stomach pains. A doctor rushed to her hotel room and he soon deduced that Mariah was in the throes of a bad case of food poisoning. There was immediate concern for her health and talk of canceling that night's performance. But ever the trooper, Mariah did not want to disappoint her fans, and insisted that the show must go on. Everyone backstage was concerned. Her road manager and members of her entourage made last-minute attempts to talk her out of performing. But Mariah stood firm — if a little bit shaky — on her decision to do the show. When she walked onstage in Atlanta, the spring was missing from her step, but Mariah was putting in a solid performance despite the illness. The consensus later was that nobody would have guessed she was sick, but the ever-truthful singer felt that the audience had the right to know why she was not able to give one hundred percent. And so, halfway through the show, she stepped up to the microphone and addressed the audience. "My manager didn't want me to tell you guys this. But I have food poisoning and am completely dehydrated, but we're going to have a good time, even if it kills me. So if I pass out, I hope somebody calls 911 for me." The announcement was greeted with momentary silence, followed by a thunderous barrage of whoops, hollers, and applause. Mariah's bravery and honesty had been rewarded. She finished the show, but her condition worsened on the flight to Boston and she was immediately rushed to Massachusetts General Hospital where she was treated for the food poisoning and dehydration over a period of several days. She recovered enough to perform in New York, but the shows in Boston and Toronto were canceled and rescheduled for late April.

Mariah finished her tour that month and was soon on a plane headed to the island of Capri, Italy where she began working in earnest on the songs for the soundtrack of her film *All That Glitters*. With the film not set to start until July, Mariah worked at a leisurely pace, enjoying the solitude and some quiet time with Luis, whose timetable was allowing him to steal away to the island of Capri for the occasional visit.

Kicking off her 2000 World Tour in Los Angeles

Those early days of the *All That Glitters* sessions were easygoing, and while on the surface it did not appear that a lot was getting done, in fact, the wide array of arrangements and vocal stylings that emerged from this time in the studio were astounding. Since *All That Glitters* was set in the eighties, Mariah found herself digging into her childhood to rediscover those funky rhythms and crisp retro licks. Prior to coming to Italy, Mariah had consulted a pair of eighties' music icons, Prince and Rick James, on the fine points of recreating that not-too-long-ago sound. Mariah took much from those conversations that filled in the blanks in an era she had grown up in and was familiar with. Consequently, there were lots of laughs and "oh yeahs" as Mariah and her music-making partners would latch onto an old riff or a style of singing and launch it into the present. Unfortunately, the peace, tranquility, and good times would not last for long.

It was nearing the time when another single from her *Rainbow* album was to be released. Mariah insisted that the third single should be "Can't Take That Away (Mariah's Theme)". It was a song that had always had a close and personal feeling for Mariah, and she felt it would translate well on the radio. But the Sony executives were not happy with her choice. They felt that something a little more upbeat, a little more in keeping with current Top Forty radio formats was necessary. The folks at Sony also realized that the success of the next single would be integral to keeping the momentum of the album going. And on this issue, Sony was not going to back down without a fight. But neither was Mariah. The ensuing arguments grew increasingly negative and angry. Mariah was taking it personally and complained bitterly to close friends that the Sony suits did not understand her or her music. But the bottom line was that Mariah was too big an artist to cross, and Sony knew that. They blinked and Mariah won. "Can't Take That Away" was finally released as a single but, as Mariah would soon discover, with drastically reduced promotion and marketing. Her victory was bittersweet because the lack of promotion would almost ensure that her song would not get the all-important radio play that would guarantee her another number one hit.

Mariah was so upset at this lack of support and, she reasoned, the deteriorating relationship with Sony since her divorce from Tommy that she took what was for her a drastic step. In late May, she began posting messages on her official website in which she chatted directly to her fans, telling them that she was receiving less-than-full support from Sony on her latest single, and that it was up to them to help her make "Can't Take That Away" a hit by calling in and requesting the song at their local radio station. One of those messages said, "Basically, a lot of you know that the political situation in my professional career is not positive. It's been really, really hard. I don't even know if this message is going to get to you because I don't know if they want you to hear this. I'm getting a lot of negative feedback from certain corporate people. But I am not willing to give up." Reaction to Mariah's clandestine messages was mixed. Her loyal fan base thought it was great and eagerly flooded their local radio stations with requests for the song. But industry observers were split on the issue. Some considered it a childish ploy that would ultimately do more harm than good. Others felt it was a bold, self-generated publicity move in an attempt to save a record she felt strongly about, but nobody doubted her sincerity.

Mariah began posting similar messages on an almost weekly basis throughout the month of June and into July. What she did not know was that the people at Sony had quickly taken notice of Mariah's attacks and would immediately strip the website, which the record company sponsored, of her messages the moment they appeared. Mariah quickly got wind of Sony's deception and fought back with the only weapon she had. She brought it to the attention of Sony corporate officials that her upcoming soundtrack album for her film *All That Glitters* was her last album on the contract she had signed with Sony back in 1990. Mariah soon began acknowledging that fact in public and began suggesting that in the wake of all the roadblocks being put in her creative path, she might not remain with Sony and was looking forward to exploring other offers. That certainly got Sony's attention, and they suddenly began showing more interest in promoting Mariah's latest single. Unfortunately, it was too little, too late. "Can't Take That Away," while doing respectable chart business, did not come close to matching her previous successes. Adding insult to injury was the knowledge that her movie *All That Glitters* was being coproduced by Columbia Pictures, the filmmaking arm of Sony Music. Mariah began to wonder how much information Columbia had on her ongoing conflicts with Sony and how their association with the record company would translate into support for her movie, which was now scheduled to begin filming in July.

For Mariah, it was the last straw. When she returned to the States after working on the *All That Glitters* soundtrack to begin preparation for filming, Mariah, according to reports, began meeting with representatives of

Arista Records, Warner Bros. Records, DreamWorks, and Elektra. The talks were merely exploratory, but Mariah's message to Sony was clear. Time was running out. Other intriguing but unsubstantiated rumors began circulating about Mariah's Sony contract. One of the most outrageous was that Mariah's contract with Sony counted for only certain studio albums, and that ones like *MTV Unplugged* and *Ones*, despite filling Sony's coffers with millions of dollars, did not count as part of the contract. The rumors were left floating out there. Nobody connected with Sony would ever comment on them, and that only succeeded in adding more fuel to the fire.

The eroding relationship between Sony and Mariah hit an all-time low midway through 2000 when the producers of the big Jim Carrey Christmas movie, *Dr. Seuss' How the Grinch Stole Christmas*, asked Mariah to compose and sing a song for the soundtrack. The problem was that the film's producer was Universal, one of Sony's arch rivals. Mariah cowrote the song "Where Are You Christmas?" and was already blocking out a period of time to record it when an edict came down from Sony saying that Mariah's contract forbade her from recording for MCA, a rival record company. An angry Mariah shot back the argument that she had already worked on other artist's albums, which made that clause in her contract invalid. Again, there were rumors that Tommy was behind this roadblock, and the stories once again began to circulate that Sony, feeling there was no chance of re-signing Mariah, was going to make her last days on the label a nightmare. But whatever the truth, legally, Mariah had no choice but to back out of the Universal soundtrack. Country singer Faith Hill was brought in to sing the Mariah composition. Hill was caught in the middle of this power struggle. She had heard all the stories about Mariah's unsuccessful attempt to sing her own song and was feeling a little guilty. But she was also grateful for the opportunity to sing a song that would almost certainly be a breakout hit. For her part, Mariah was gracious, and although she was angry that she could not sing her own song, she was appreciative that at least somebody with considerable talent would do it right.

Meanwhile, the Sony power struggle over *Rainbow* continued. The critical response to the cover song "Against All Odds (Take a Look at Me Now)" had been positive, and the consensus was that it would be a good next single. Mariah agreed, but rather than simply release an edited version of the album cut, she had a more progressive idea. She was a fan of the up-and-coming Irish pop group Westlife and felt redoing the tune with them would give the song a real commercial edge. The group was thrilled with the opportunity, and a rehearsal session was set up in a studio in Ireland. On the surface, the session went quite smoothly and everybody was happy with the song and the resultant video. With the help of an engineer, Mariah produced the session herself. The members of Westlife recalled that they had a huge case of nerves on the day they arrived to record the song, so much so that the band decided to have a drink to settle themselves before the session, and they adjourned to the hotel bar. On the day in question, the members of Westlife were sitting in the bar downing drinks when who should walk in but Mariah herself. The singer promptly joined the group, and according to Westlife's Bryan McFadden, "We had a few drinks and everybody relaxed. Mariah even got a bit tipsy."

But the good-time nature of the session changed according to a Mariah Carey interview with MTV Asia not long after the session was completed. "The whole thing wasn't a drama or anything, but even though they're just starting out, they can get a little egotistical." Westlife shot back with charges that the "Against All Odds" video shoot was the worst experience the band had ever had. The resulting video had to be reedited when it was discovered that band member Bryan McFadden was paying a bit too much attention to Mariah's cleavage. Mariah was disappointed at the backbiting in the aftermath of the session but insisted that the resulting song was great and would most certainly be a hit.

Mariah's growing prowess as an actress, despite making only a token appearance in *The Bachelor*, was continuing to draw interest from the Hollywood community. It had got to the point where she was being seriously mentioned for starring roles in other high-profile movies. During this period, high-powered producer Joel Silver, who was behind such smash hits as the *Lethal Weapon* movies, suggested that Mariah might be good in the title role for his projected movie based on the *Wonder Woman* comic book. Mariah was reportedly delighted by the offer and said that she would consider it. There was also talk that Mariah would be perfect for the starring role in the proposed remake of *A Star Is Born*, but that suggestion, by Hollywood standards, was way too premature. The rumor also began to circulate that Mariah was about to sign a deal to star in the critically acclaimed Broadway musical *Les Misérables*.

Mariah was continuing to get up to speed on the production side of making a movie and, in the process, had heard more than one story of a film stopped dead in its tracks when something unexpected happened to its star. And so she purchased a ten-million-dollar insurance policy on herself in case of an injury on the set. She had a good laugh at the notion that something might actually happen to her, but she was taking producing and starring in a film very seriously. Therefore, she was taking no chances. Shortly before going to Toronto to begin filming *All That Glitters*, Mariah received the exciting news that Da Brat and respected musician Eric Benet had landed roles in the movie. This was comforting to Mariah who had begun to develop a bit of uneasiness in the days leading up to the start of filming. With the addition of her musical friends, the film set was beginning to take on the ambiance of a concert stage or a recording studio — two places in which she felt most confident and most in control.

Her early meetings with the movie's director Vondie Curtis-Hall had been encouraging. Curtis-Hall, a veteran actor and director, who had most recently worked on the television series *Chicago Hope*, had an instinct for newcomers, and he assured Mariah that everything would turn out fine. With Curtis-Hall and the film's other producers helping her, Mariah's confidence grew as she learned firsthand what goes into making a movie. Mariah was a quick and enthusiastic study in such areas as casting and budgeting and took to the process with the same sense of excitement and enthusiasm that she brought to the recording studio. Mariah was also quite happy with the final draft of the script. Equal parts *A Star Is Born* and not-too-disguised aspects of her own life, *All That Glitters* was big on character, flash, realism, and, of course, music — all the elements that Mariah felt were necessary for her first starring role to be a success.

It rained the first two days of filming in Toronto, and *All That Glitters* was immediately behind schedule. But that did not worry Mariah, who was completely caught up in the fantasy as well as the reality of being on the soundstage or the outdoor location of a movie. When she was working, she was putting her heart and soul into every scene, no matter how minor. Those on the set during those first few days quickly got over their admitted apprehension about an untried pop music star attempting to make the transition to acting because what they were seeing in Mariah was somebody who took direction well, was anxious to learn, and who was not above asking questions.

Those early scenes, with the outskirts of Toronto doubling for the Georgia countryside in which part of the film takes place, showcased

Mariah as an actress of surprising depth and emotion. An argument could be made for the fact that she was essentially playing herself, but the singer-turned-actress would later admit that the character and what she brought to it was something totally new. "I really enjoy the process of acting," she said in an *Entertainment Tonight* interview. "The whole process of making a movie has helped me grow as a person."

When she was not acting, Mariah was enjoying her off time in Toronto. Her days were spent shopping, and she reportedly bought so many clothes that she had to book two additional hotel rooms just to handle her purchases. Off camera, Mariah was also friendly with cast and crew members and spent many nights partying at local clubs with them. She was not the type to shut herself off in her trailer when not working and would routinely be found talking and joking with fellow actors, makeup people, and others.

In particular, Mariah had developed a close friendship with costar Eric Benet, and to nobody's surprise, the tabloids had a field day with that. They exploded with headlines about Mariah and Eric (who at the time was hot and heavy with actress Halle Berry) getting romantic on the set of the film. There wasn't a word of truth in it, but it was par for the course. It was to be expected, and Mariah and Eric were used to it. So they simply laughed it off. But the rumors persisted, becoming more outlandish and vicious. Stories began to circulate that Halle Berry had come to the set and had angrily confronted Mariah. It was also reported that Luis Miguel, who was coming to the Toronto site every chance he could to be with his love, was upset by the reports and that the alleged dalliance with Benet was putting a serious crimp in their relationship. Mariah felt she finally had to address the rumors. "There has been a whole bunch of ridiculous press that Eric and I are in some kind of love fest. It's a complete lie."

Mariah's creative life took another hit when another lawsit was filed in September by songwriters Seth Swirsky and Warren Cambell, who claimed that Mariah's song "Thank God I Found You" borrowed heavily from their song "One Of Those Love Songs," which was recorded by the group Xscape in 1998. Once again, Mariah vehemently denied the plagiarism charge and defended herself in court.

While Mariah labored in front of the camera, producers Jimmy Jam and Terry Lewis continued to pull together music for the *All That Glitters* soundtrack. What had started out as six songs to be sprinkled throughout the film had quickly evolved into an even dozen in various stages of production. "We were basically writing new music as the movie evolved," Jam told MTV. "When Eric Benet was added to the cast of the film, we decided that it might be a good idea to have a duet between Mariah and Eric, so we added another song. A lot of times, we would get on the phone with Mariah, and she would say, 'I need another track for such and such a scene,' and we would just turn it around for her."

In September, the *All That Glitters* production moved to New York where the more emotional and romantic aspects of the fictional storyline would unfold. Mariah continued to draw praise for the wide array of emotions she displayed in the film and her growing prowess as a producer behind the camera. Mariah was quietly confident that she was getting the job done. "It's been good," she told MTV after a particularly grueling night shoot. "It's like a little, secluded cocoon world where I quite enjoy not dealing with reality." Director Vondie Curtis-Hall continued to be one of Mariah's biggest supporters. "She worked really hard for it," he said during the editing stage of *All That Glitters*. "She did a lot of preparation. I think she had a lot to prove. I gave her as much direction as I could. I just sort of guided her in an area I thought would best support her character."

However, reality continued to intrude on her "secluded cocoon world." Sony Records was now in a full-blown panic. There had been some tentative attempts to pin Mariah down about her contract, but any questions about what her future dealings with Sony would be got sidetracked. All they could get was that Mariah would actively promote the coming film and the soundtrack. Anything beyond that was shrouded in mystery and silence. Of course that didn't stop the rumors. The one that seemed closest to reality was that Mariah had not decided to leave Sony yet but would use the *All That Glitters* movie and soundtrack as a barometer of how much the label wanted her to stay. If they did not market both to number one, she was gone. Another story making the rounds was that Mariah was all but signed with Arista, based largely on the way they had resurrected the career of Carlos Santana. This account claimed that she was just stringing Sony along in an attempt to get even for all the perceived slights of the past decade. One thing was certain. And that was that only Mariah knew what she was going to do next.

CHAPTER TWELVE

Into the Future

Mariah walked into New York's famed Limelight Club in mid-October. There was a sense of pride and accomplishment on her face as she conferred with director Curtis-Hall about the night's sequences. This would be the last night of shooting on *All That Glitters*. And to her way of thinking, Mariah had come through the challenge with flying colors. Her first film as producer and star had come in on time and on budget, a true rarity in Hollywood.

Mariah was immediately taken on a much-needed vacation by Luis. The couple went south of the border to Mexico and then to Barbados where they lived the good life. The pair were so assured of the strength of their relationship that they laughed off the constant scrutiny by the tabloid press. They ignored the paparazzi as they spent their time in the finest clubs, restaurants, and most importantly, alone, away from prying eyes.

Mariah returned to the United States emotionally and spiritually invigorated and, not surprisingly, anxious to jump into an endless round of postproduction work on the movie and the soundtrack. Mariah supervised much of the editing being done by director Vondie Curtis-Hall. The give-and-take was much like the rapport that she had developed with the producers of her albums over the years. But there was a slight difference here: Mariah was an old hand in the recording studio but not in the film studio. So she would limit herself to offering suggestions on what she considered a good take or a closeup she felt was particularly flattering, but in the end, the bottom line was always to go with her instincts, which was to trust

Curtis-Hall because he obviously knew more about the process than Mariah did. As he went over the completed footage that would ultimately become *All That Glitters*, director Curtis-Hall was even more confident that this was going to be Mariah's breakout performance. "I know what you're thinking," Curtis-Hall said in an interview. "Another pop star trying to act. But a lot of you are going to be surprised."

Back in the recording studio working on the soundtrack, Mariah felt a glorious rush of adrenaline. She was in her element again, and the excitement was instantly evident. Fragments of material that were created while Mariah was making the movie were soon fleshed out with taut arrangements and Mariah's inspired vocals. Those around Mariah in the studio had expected a bit of a letdown following the months making *All That Glitters*, but what they discovered was that the singer was now totally energized and ready to take her talents to even greater heights. If *All That Glitters* did turn out to be her last album for Sony, the label would be the recipient of her finest effort. "Against All Odds (Take a Look at Me Now)" was released worldwide in October and all animosity between Mariah and Westlife was forgotten as the record quickly began its climb up the charts in Europe, Asia, South America, and the United States. It made it into the top five in several countries. This chart activity came as a welcome relief to Mariah watchers. The previous couple of years had seen the advent of megastar pop teens such as Christina Aguilera and Britney Spears, and some were saying that Mariah's pop-diva persona was out of fashion, and that her career would most certainly decline as the competition for radio play became more fierce. Mariah welcomed the competition and insisted that her career was far from over.

Mariah's musical aspirations continued to be far-reaching. The singer's growing desire to work on other people's albums resulted in her popping into the studio to do some backup singing on the Babyface song "Every Time I Close My Eyes." Word was also out that Mariah was taking Spanish lessons with an eye toward singing a couple of Spanish-language songs, possibly with lover Luis Miguel, on her next album. But Mariah, perhaps still smarting from the failure of their previous attempt to record a duet for *Rainbow* remained cautious on that subject. "We do sing together in private," she explained to the *New York Daily News*. "That's much more important to me than trying to exploit a relationship by doing a duet."

Word along the music-industry grapevine continued to be that Mariah's

All That Glitters soundtrack was so good and contained so many potential hit singles that rather than release the first song simultaneously with the film, they wanted to maximize the album's potential by releasing the first single well in advance of the movie. The rumor mill soon began spinning with the news that the first single, yet to be determined, would be released in January 2001, nearly three months ahead of the projected date that *All That Glitters* would appear in theaters. That bit of news was barely out of the box when an even more surprising item came out of the annual meeting of Sam Goody record company managers in Atlanta, Georgia. The giant retail chain reported that Mariah was planning to release an album in January or February of 2001. According to reports coming out of the manager's conference, the album would consist of leftover tracks from previous albums and alternate takes of familiar songs, and was Mariah's attempt to give Sony the final album on her contract without trusting them to do right with what she considered the all-important *All That Glitters* soundtrack. Of course, this news set the rumor mills humming. Immediately the story started making the rounds that Mariah had, in fact, already nailed down an agreement with a new label, and that her soundtrack album would be the first album of her new deal. Typical of this kind of blockbuster announcement, nobody was admitting to anything, including Mariah.

Into the fall and winter months, Mariah found herself in an all-too-familiar whirlwind of activity. There was the constant demands of the up-coming film and soundtrack album. The buzz on her performance in *All That Glitters* had led to other acting offers, which she was considering. But, for the most part, the final months of 2000 were turning into a rather contemplative time for Mariah. November brought two small glimpses of Mariah to the public when *The Grinch* soundtrack, featuring Mariah's song and Babyface's new greatest hits album with Mariah as background singer, hit the bricks. There was a lot she could or should be doing, but Mariah did not seem in any hurry to make a decision. While not completely surrendering to play, the singer did seem to be enjoying a period in her life that was not making any major demands. She was finding more and more time to be with Luis — a romance that was beginning to look like the real thing. There were the joyous times with her mother and her friends. And finally, there were the times to look back on her life and her career.

From a commercial perspective, the nineties belonged to Mariah. Her music was a mainstay on the album charts and radio playlists, and there are signs that this will continue. Far from a one-note performer, Mariah has grown as a producer and actor, moving in a number of different directions that will undoubtedly keep her in high profile for years to come and away from the possibility of oversaturation in one area. There are those who claim that Mariah's career owes more to luck and timing than outstanding skills, and that her early studio-bound years continue to haunt her with the tag of bland pop diva. But don't tell that to her fans who have spent the past decade living vicariously through her words and her music. Longevity is no accident. It is the byproduct of persistence, talent, and an overwhelming desire to be the best performer in the world. The jury is out on whether she is that, but nobody can argue with her level of success.

Personally, Mariah remains on a road of self-discovery. She is still very much the woman-child — still admittedly naive in the ways of love and romance but secure in a relationship that remains strong. Mariah has always been vague about her intentions for the future. Right now marriage and children are still a way off, but her longstanding unease about a second marriage has been replaced by a resolve to someday make it all work. It has not been easy. It will never be perfect. And, of course, there are some things she probably would have done differently. But warts and all, this has been Mariah Carey's real life.

Stay tuned for the future.

Epilogue

. . . And so, as Mariah Carey stood on stage in Las Vegas and listened to the thunderous applause while accepting the Artist of the Decade Award at the Billboard Music Award ceremony, she reflected on how much this award meant to her. For Mariah, winning this award was indeed a dream come true, a culmination of all her hard work. Mariah had been asked to sing at the ceremony, and she was happy to perform even though she was a bit tentative regarding award shows in general, given her previous Grammy slights. So, Mariah was expecting nothing more than a good time. But she was positively shocked and elated when, at the end of the evening, she was awarded the ultimate honor of Artist of the Decade Award.

After the ceremony and the expected round of gladhanding with superstars and record-company executives who lined up to congratulate her, Mariah and a close friend, singer Trey Lorenz, who was standing in for Mariah's true love, Luis Miguel, jumped into a limo and headed for an out-of-the-way restaurant for a late-night dinner. As she walked through the restaurant, Mariah and Trey passed a table where a woman was throwing a lavish birthday party for her boyfriend. The woman spotted Mariah and raced over, excitedly begging the superstar to sing "Happy Birthday" to her boyfriend. Mariah graciously agreed and with the help of her friend, sang an impromptu *a capella* "Happy Birthday" to the woman's astonished boyfriend.

Mariah barely beat the sunrise back to her hotel room. When she arrived, she was overjoyed to find seven dozen red roses and a congratulatory note from her lover, Latin heartthrob Luis Miguel, who was currently on tour on the other side of the world. "I had this really great night," she would explain to *Rolling Stone*. "For once, I had this really great, triumphant feeling about the whole thing." For once? Wasn't this a person who had it all? Had not the perks of stardom and public adulation on a worldwide level been a joy all along? Not really. For the veil has been lifting since 1997, and the secrets have been creeping out.

Mariah, in her most candid moments, has admitted that there was a lot that was good, perhaps even joyous, in the decade just concluded. Her arrival as one of the top singers on the planet was a dream come true. But she has also been candid in revealing that she was literally a puppet on a string during much of those years — controlled, manipulated, and not too subtly pressured into living her life by a code of conduct that was not really hers. She felt like a pawn to personal and corporate entities who claimed to have her best interests at heart but were actually seeing her as a living, breathing bottom line. Mariah was not completely blind to what was going on around her, but then those were the days when she was still a child, and she felt powerless to fight back. "There have been people in my life who have broken my heart," she once told an interviewer. "But I don't want to give anyone the credit."

Mariah's life has changed drastically in the past three years since her much-publicized divorce from record-company mogul Tommy Mottola. Before then, the woman in the restaurant would have been intercepted by Mariah's army of ever-present and overzealous bodyguards before she could have made her "Happy Birthday" request. Now, Mariah has come to grips with the importance of the balance of stability and freedom in her personal and professional life. The singer has become very hands-on in piloting the fortunes of her most recent albums — *Butterfly*, *Rainbow*, and *All That Glitters*. Rather than caving in to the demands that she play it safe, bland, and middle of the road, Mariah has defiantly flown in the face of prevailing wisdom when she added elements of hip-hop and rap to her normally polished, mellow, middle-of-the-road sound and made the daring experiment work. "In this world, I call the shots," she told a *Glamour* magazine reporter. "And I think I know best."

The flowers from Luis Miguel? Three years ago, Mariah would not have been ready for true love. But now, going into the year 2001, Mariah

Mariah receives the Billboard Music Award for Artist of the Decade
EVERETT COLLECTION

Carey has found a new life. Mariah Carey recently turned thirty, and the little girl has finally grown up. But in her personal life, Mariah is still very much the young girl, indulging the simple pleasures of hanging out in clubs with her girlfriends, driving down the street with the radio blasting, and, yes, even falling in love — despite the constant glare of the spotlight. It hasn't been easy but, again, she's made it work.

For Mariah, the complexities and challenges of growing up have been many and seem, on the surface, to have been insurmountable. A literal woman–child, Mariah was thrust into the very-adult world of show business barely a year out of high school. Compounding the insecurities of a nomadic, flawed childhood, Mariah was being asked to trust strangers before she truly knew the meaning of the word. And while she seemed assured on the concert stage or in the studio putting her high multioctave voice to natural, heartfelt words, the reality was "I was tiptoeing around things all my life." And, to a large degree, she still is. Because the demons have been slow to leave.

As recently as 1999, as part of an exercise with her acting teacher, Mariah was asked to imagine a time and place in which she felt most secure. Mariah tried and tried, but the image would not come. She later reasoned that it was because she had never felt truly secure. That was truly an eye-opener, and that realization gave a sense of positive urgency to the new Mariah Carey. In her mind, she is making up for lost time, and so there is, to the outside observer, an often dizzy, confusing, near-frantic spur-of-the-moment feel to the way she is conducting her life. There seems to be no rhyme nor reason to Mariah in the year 2000. She has admitted to not sleeping much in recent years, preferring to spend all hours of the day and night refining her music and taking her life day by day and in which ever direction the wind blows.

Typical of Mariah's current flights of fancy was the recent announcement that she was considering kicking off her projected next world tour in, of all places, Guam. According to the *New York Daily News* and *Rolling Stone*, she went so far as to pay a visit to Guam and talk seriously with local officials about a concert that would end with her releasing a flock of pigeons into the heavens. Her reasoning was that she had suddenly developed a mystical connection with the word "Guam."

There have also been times when Mariah "does not realize where she is at any given moment." More than one pundit has hinted that she is a classic case of over-compensation for an early life that was largely directed and controlled by others. And who can say that she is not justified in feeling the need to make up for lost time? "I don't feel like I've lived a lot of things that were going on," she said in a candid *Trace* magazine interview. "I don't feel like I really experienced things the same way that I'm experiencing things that go on now."

But those close to her steadfastly believe that Mariah's current high-speed life is a joyous coming out rather than a detriment. Longtime friend Trey Lorenz has stated that "people are actually now seeing the cool side of Mariah, the person who is just like you and me." Patricia Carey, Mariah's mother, readily acknowledges that her daughter is now "more content with herself, and there's a peace that she has now."

Mariah, who in recent years, has alternated between saying nothing and being enticingly cryptic when it has come to her personal trials and tribulations, once summed up the roller coaster that has been her life when she told a *Rolling Stone* reporter "For me to get to this point, it took an enormous amount of strength." But being candid is still a tenuous position for the singer, one that still has Mariah on her guard. "I go around consciously trying to maintain in a world that's a little bit crazy," she told *Trace*. "I love the fact that now I'm able to do what I want."

Where this new chapter in her life will take her is anybody's guess. The multiplatinum success of *Rainbow* and its subsequent SRO American tour made it plain that Mariah's creative instincts remain intact and that her growing business acumen will not allow her to be taken advantage of anymore. Her long-held interest in acting also seems to be flowering. After a tentative but successful cameo appearance in the 1999 film *The Bachelor*, she was encouraged to take the next step — a starring role in the semi-autobiographical story of an up-and-coming eighties pop singer, entitled *All That Glitters*, which was filmed in the summer and fall of 2000 and will hopefully be released in 2001.

Mariah also seems secure now in her personal life. Her most serious post-divorce relationship, prior to Luis Miguel, with New York Yankee baseball player Derek Jeter began and ended in the blink of an eye. That she weathered it emotionally and was able to move on quickly said much about her maturity and toughness when it came to affairs of the heart. And her relationship with Miguel has been a risk. The entertainment industry is littered with the remains of failed relationships between superstars. But so far, Mariah and Luis are proving that love can truly conquer all.

Yes there are those intangibles. The kinds of things that drive skeptics and fans alike to speculate on what the future may bring for the reborn Mariah Carey. Can a personality alternately so strong and yet so vulnerable survive in an often-cutthroat music industry? Or will it all ultimately become too much, forcing Mariah into a Barbra Streisand-like existence of only occasional recordings and even rarer public appearances? Will her current love last, and if not, will she ever find love or be doomed to a series of short-term relationships?

There will be many more questions as the years go by, and Mariah has admitted, on more than one occasion, that she may not have all the answers. But Mariah Carey has the advantage of thirty years of history and experience to draw upon in dealing with whatever the future may bring. And she is not afraid. "I've gone through a lot of stuff and that got me to the next level," she said in an online chat. "It's all pretty basic. You evolve. You grow up."

And so, Mariah Carey has arrived in the year 2001 at the top of her game and her life, and her music continues to captivate the hearts and minds of millions. She has moved into the future. And it is a future filled with dreams — dreams that will certainly come true!

MANY THANKS

To my wife Nancy and daughter Rachael for the love, support, and all the good stuff that keeps me sane. My agent Lori Perkins who has dedicated much of her life to keeping me working 24-7. Robert Lecker and the good people at ECW. My mom Selma Howe. Bennie and Freda. Mike Kirby, Steve Ross, and all the boys in the hood. Kerri, Bad Baby, Chaos, and all the animals in the hood. Good books, good music, and good art. And finally, thanks for a profession that keeps those surprises coming.

DISCOGRAPHY

ALBUMS

MARIAH CAREY
(1990)
SONGS: Vision of Love, There's Got to Be a Way, I Don't Wanna Cry, Someday, Vanishing, All in Your Mind, Alone in Love, You Need Me, Sent From Up Above, Prisoner, Love Takes Time

EMOTIONS
(1991)
SONGS: Emotions, And You Don't Remember, Can't Let Go, Make It Happen, If It's Over, You're So Cold, So Blessed, To Be Around You, Till the End of Time, The Wind

MTV UNPLUGGED EP
(1992)
SONGS: Emotions, If It's Over, Someday, Vision of Love, Make It Happen, I'll Be There, Can't Let Go

MUSIC BOX
(1993)
SONGS: Dreamlover, Hero, Anytime You Need a Friend, Music Box, Now That I Know, Never Forget You, Without You, Just to Hold You Once Again, I've Been Thinking About You, All I've Ever Wanted

MERRY CHRISTMAS

(1994)

SONGS: Silent Night, All I Want for Christmas Is You, O Holy Night, Christmas (Baby Please Come Home), Miss You Most (At Christmas Time), Joy to the World, Jesus Born on This Day, Santa Claus Is Comin' to Town, Hark! The Herald Angels Sing/Gloria (In Excelsis Deo), Jesus Oh What a Wonderful Child

DAYDREAM

(1995)

SONGS: Fantasy, Underneath the Stars, One Sweet Day, Open Arms, Always Be My Baby, I Am Free, When I Saw You, Long Ago, Melt Away, Forever, Daydream Interlude (Fantasy Sweet Dub Mix), Looking In

BUTTERFLY

(1997)

SONGS: Honey, Butterfly, My All, The Roof, Fourth of July, Breakdown, Babydoll, Close My Eyes, Whenever You Call, Fly Away (Butterfly Reprise), The Beautiful Ones, Outside

#1's

(1998)

SONGS: Vision of Love, Love Takes Time, Someday, I Don't Wanna Cry, Emotions, I'll Be There [Featuring Trey Lorenz], Dreamlover, Hero, Fantasy [Featuring O.D.B.], One Sweet Day [Mariah Carey & Boyz II Men], Always Be My Baby, Honey, My All, Sweetheart [Mariah Featuring JD], When You Believe (From *The Prince of Egypt*) [Mariah Carey & Whitney Houston], Whenever You Call [Mariah Carey & Brian McKnight], I Still Believe

RAINBOW

(1999)

SONGS: Heartbreaker, Can't Take That Away (Mariah's Theme), Bliss, How Much, After Tonight, X-Girlfriend, Heartbreaker (Remix), Vulnerability (Interlude), Against All Odds (Take a Look at Me Now), Crybaby, Did I Do That?, Petals, Rainbow (Interlude), Thank God I Found You

SINGLES

1990
Vision of Love
Love Takes Time

1991
Someday
I Don't Wanna Cry
There's Got to Be a Way [Europe Only]
Emotions
Can't Let Go

1992
Make It Happen
I'll Be There
If It's Over [Europe Only]

1993
Dreamlover
Hero

1994
Without You
Never Forget You
Anytime You Need a Friend
Endless Love [with Luther Vandross]
All I Want for Christmas Is You [released in 1994 and 1996]
Jesus Born on This Day [promotional single only]
Joy to the World [released in 1994 and 1995]
Miss You Most (At Christmas Time)

1995
Fantasy
One Sweet Day [with Boyz II Men]

1996
Open Arms [not released in the United States and Japan]
Always Be My Baby
Forever [not released in the United States and Japan]
Underneath the Stars [promotional single only]
O Holy Night [promotional single only]

1997
Honey
Butterfly

1998
Breakdown
The Roof (Back in Time) [released in Europe only]
My All
Sweetheart [with Jermaine Dupri]
When You Believe [with Whitney Houston]
A Natural Woman [with Céline Dion, Gloria Estefan, Shania Twain, Aretha Franklin, and Carole King]

1999
I Still Believe
Do You Know Where You're Going To [promotional single only]
Heartbreaker

2000
Thank God I Found You
Valentines [only available at Wal-Mart stores]
Against All Odds (Take a Look at Me Now) [with Westlife]
Can't Take That Away (Mariah's Theme)
Crybaby [promotional single]

VIDEOGRAPHY

1990

Vision of Love
Length: 3:30
Director: Bojan Bazelli

Love Takes Time
Length: 3:50
Director: Jeb Bien and Walter Maser

1991

Someday
Length: 3:36
Director: Larry Jordan

I Don't Wanna Cry
Length: 4:50
Director: Jeb Bien

There's Got to Be a Way
Length: 4:54
Director: Info not available

Emotions
Length: 4:08
Director: Jeff Preiss

Can't Let Go
Length: 4:28
Director: Jim Sonzero

1992

Make It Happen
Length: 5:08
Director: Marcus Nispel

I'll Be There
Length: 4:43
Director: Larry Jordan

If It's Over
Length: 3:48
Director: Larry Jordan

1993

Dreamlover
Length: 3:54
Director: Diane Martel

Hero
Length: 4:20
Director: Larry Jordan

1994

Without You
Length: 3:36
Director: Larry Jordan

Anytime You Need a Friend
Length: 4:26-6:15 remix
Director: D. Federici

All I Want for Christmas Is You
Length: 3:35
Director: Diane Martel

Miss You Most (At Christmas Time)
Length: 3:35
Director: Diane Martel

Joy to the World
Length: 4:21
Director: Info not available

Endless Love
Length:
Director: Info not available

1995

Fantasy
Length: 4:04
Director: Mariah Carey

One Sweet Day
Length: 4:43
Director: Larry Jordan

1996

Open Arms
Length: 3:35
Director: Info not available

Always Be My Baby
Length: 4:21
Director: Mariah Carey

Forever
Length: 4:01
Director: Larry Jordan

1997

Honey
Length: 6:41
Director: Paul Hunter and Daniel Pearl

Butterfly
Length: 4:35
Director: Daniel Pearl and Mariah Carey

The Roof
Length: 5:34
Director: Mariah Carey and Diane
    Martel

Breakdown
Length: 4:32
Director: Mariah Carey and Diane
    Martel

1998

My All
Length: 3:56
Director: Herb Ritts

My All — Stay Awhile (hip-hop remix)
Length: 4:16
Director: Diane Martel

Whenever You Call
Length: 4:24
Director: Info not available

Sweetheart
Length: 4:30
Director: Hype Williams

When You Believe
Length: 4:36
Director: Phil Joanou

1999

I Still Believe
Length: 3:55
Director: Brett Ratner

I Still Believe (Damizzia remix)
Length: Info not available
Director: Mariah Carey

Heartbreaker
Length: 4:26
Director: Brett Ratner

Heartbreaker (remix)
Length: 4:26
Director: Diane Martel

Thank God I Found You
Length: Info not available
Director: Info not available

Thank God I Found You (make it last remix)
Length: Info not available
Director: Info not available

2000

Crybaby
Length: Info not available
Director: Info not available

Against All Odds
Length: Info not available
Director: Info not available

Can't Take That Away
Length: Info not available
Director: Info not available

Against All Odds [with Westlife]
Length: Info not available
Director: Info not available

GUEST APPEARANCES

As Singer

Luther Vandross
Songs
"Endless Love"

Babyface
The Day
"Everytime I Close My Eyes"

Men in Black
The Soundtrack
"I Can Make You Happy" [with Trey Lorenz]

Princess Diana Tribute Album
"Hero" [live, unreleased version]

J.D.
Life in 1472
"Sweetheart"

Divas Live
VH-1 Divas Live
"Chain of Fools" [with Aretha Franklin]
"My All"
"Make It Happen"

Whitney Houston
My Love Is Your Love
"When You Believe" [with Whitney Houston]

The Prince of Egypt Soundtrack
"When You Believe" [with Whitney Houston]

Funkmaster Flex
Volume III
"Freestyle Pt. II" [featuring The League]

Patti LaBelle
Live! One Night Only
"Got to Be Real" [with Patti LaBelle]

Luciano Pavarotti
Pavarotti and Friends
"Hero" [duet with Luciano Pavarotti]
"My All"

Songwriter and Producer

Trey Lorenz
Trey Lorenz
"Someone to Hold" (lyrics and coproduction)
"Always in Love" (lyrics and coproduction)

Trey Lorenz
12 Soulful Nights of Christmas
"My Younger Days" (lyrics and production)

Daryl Hall
Soul Alone
"Help Me Find a Way to Your Heart" (lyrics)

Allure
Allure
"Head Over Heels" (lyrics)
"Last Chance" (lyrics)

7 Miles
7 Miles
"After" (lyrics and production)

Blaque
Blaque
"Don't Go Looking for Love" (lyrics and production)

AWARDS

GRAMMY AWARDS

1991
Best Pop Vocal Performance
Best New Artist

BILLBOARD AWARDS

1991
Top Adult Contemporary Artist
Top Pop Artist
Top Album Artist
Top Pop Album Artist
Top Pop Singles Artist
Top Pop Singles Artist — Female

1992
Top Female Album Artist
Top Female Singles Artist

1994
Female Artist of the Year

1996
Special Award: Chart Performance
Hot 100 Singles Artist of the Year
Hot 100 Airplay
Hot Adult Contemporary Artist of the Year

1998
Special Hot 100 Award

1999
Female Artist of the Decade in the 1990s

WORLD MUSIC AWARDS

1995
World's Best-Selling Pop Artist
World's Best American Recording Artist
World's Overall Best-Performing Artist

1996
World's Best-Selling R&B Female Artist of the Year
World's Best-Selling Pop Artist of the Year
World's Best-Selling American Female Artist of the Year
World's Best-Selling Overall Recording Female Artist of the Year

1998
World's Best-Selling R&B Artist
World's Best-Selling Recording Artist of the 90s

2000
Best-Selling Pop Female Artist of the Millennium

BMI MUSIC AWARDS

1991
Song of the Year

1996
Song of the Year

1997
Song of the Year

1998
Song of the Year
1999
Pop Songwriter of the Year

SOUL TRAIN MUSIC AWARDS

1990
Best New R&B/Urban Contemporary Artist
Best New R&B/ Urban Contemporary Single
Best New R&B/Urban Contemporary Album

1998
Aretha Franklin Award for Entertainer of the Year
Soul Train Lady of Soul Award

AMERICAN MUSIC AWARDS

1992
Favorite Soul/ R&B Artist

1993
Favorite Pop/Rock Female Artist
Favorite Adult Contemporary Album

1995
Favorite Pop/Rock Female Artist

1996
Favorite Pop/Rock Female Artist
Favorite Soul/R&B Female Artist

1998
Favorite Soul/R&B Female Artist

2000
Special Award for Having A #1 Single Every Year of the 90s

BIBLIOGRAPHY

BOOKS

Jeter, Derek with Jack Curry. *The Life You Imagine: Life Lessons for Achieving Your Dreams*. New York: Crown, 2000.

Nickson, Chris. *Mariah Carey Revisited: The Unauthorized Biography*, New York: St. Martins-Griffin, 1998.

White, Timothy. *Music To My Ears: The Billboard Essays: Award-Winning Portraits of Popular Music In the '90s*. New York: Henry Holt, 1997.

Current Biography Yearbook, 1992.

TELEVISION SHOWS

The Today Show (Australian T.V.), 1996.

The Donnie and Marie Show, December 1998.

The Charlie Rose Show, November 1999.

The Oprah Winfrey Show, November 1999.

The Rosie O'Donnell Show, February 1999.

MAGAZINE AND NEWSPAPER ARTICLES

Anson, Robert Sam. "Tommy Boy." *Vanity Fair*, November 1996.

Arrington, Carl. "Queen of the High C's." *TV Guide*, 1993.

Chambers, Veronica. "Mariah on Fire." *Newsweek*, November 15, 1999.

Considine, J. D. "A Rainbow for Mariah Carey." *Baltimore Sun*, October 31, 1999.

Croft, Lara. "The Story of the Pop Cinderella." *Spiegel*, November 1999.

Davies, David. "The Q Interview." *Q*, November 1997.

Dell, Pamela. "The Divine Miss Mariah." *Teen*, July 1993.

Dougherty, Steve. "A Butterfly Takes Wing." *People*, February, 1998.

—. "How Sweet It Is." *People*, November, 1993.

Dunn, Jancee. "The US Interview." *US*, October 1993.

Edwards, Steve. "Sweet Mariah." *Rotations*, January 1997.

Ehrlich, Dimitri. "Mariah's Magic." *Courier-Mail*, October, 1999.

—. "Interview With Mariah Carey." *Interview*, September 1999.

Farley, Christopher John. "Pop's Princess Grows Up." *Time*, 1995.

Gardner, Elysa. "Calling the Shots Solo." *Los Angeles Times*, September 1997.

—. "Cinderella Story." *Vibe*, April 1996.

—. "For Mariah a Life That Glitters." *USA Today*, November 2, 1999.

Goodman, Fred. "The Marketing Muscle Behind Mariah Carey." *New York Times*, April 14, 1991.

Gundersen, Edna. "The Voice of Emotions: Mariah Carey Digs Deep for a Heartfelt Second Album." *USA Today*, September 9, 1991.

Handelman, David. "Miss Mariah." *Cosmopolitan*, December 1997.

Harrington, Richard. "A Real Live Fantasy, Mariah Carey Didn't Climb to the Top, She Soared." *Washington Post*, November 19, 1995.

Herman, James Patrick. "Even Posthumously She Remains Drop Dead Gorgeous." *Mirabella*, April 1999.

Holden, Stephen. "The Pop Gospel According to Mariah Carey." *New York Times*, September 5, 1991.

Johannesson, Ika. "Free to Play Sexy Diva." *Dagens Nyheter*, April, 1999.

Johnson, Robert E. "My Mom Taught Me How to Believe in Myself." *Jet*, January 1994.

Kvarnng, Magdalena. "Interview With Mariah." *Aftonbladet*, January 1999.

Linden, Amy. "Carry on Baggage." *VH1's The Score*, April 6, 1998.

M., Rudi. "Honey-Voiced Mariah Breaks Loose." *Black Beat*, August 1997.

Mason, Leslee. "Is Mariah Understood?" *Modern Woman*, December 1997.

Navarro, Juan Manuel. "Thank God She Has Found Luis." *Gente*, November 1999.

Norment, Lynn. "Mariah Carey." *Ebony*, April 1994.

—. "Not Another White Girl Trying to Sing Black." *Ebony*, March 1991.

Olovsson, Ronny. "Mariah Makes a Movie About Her Childhood and Growth." November 1997.

Pener, Degen. "Butterflies Aren't Free." *Entertainment Weekly*, September, 1997.

Rottenberg, Josh. "Much, Much More Mariah." *Glamour*, November 1999.

S. Bam. "Interview With Mariah Carey." *Bild Am Sonntag*, October 1999.

Smith, Liz. "Mariah Carey Stretched to the Max." *Toronto Sun*, June 22, 1997.

Sutcliffe, Phil. "Mariah Carey." *Q*, June 1994.

Tannenbaum, Rob. "Building the Perfect Diva." August 23, 1990.

Thigpen, David E. "Butterflies Are Free." *Time*, September 1997.

Udovitch, Mimi. "An Unmarried Woman." *Rolling Stone*, May 1998.

—. "The Whirling Diva." *Rolling Stone*, February, 2000.

Villasimil, Alejandra. "Mariah Carey Affirms That Her Heart Has Been Broken Many Times." *Notimex*, September 1999.

Williams, Jeannie. "News and Views." *USA Today*, November 11, 1997.

Williston, Beverly. "The Truth About Me and Men." *Star*, October, 1997.